An Invitation to My Heart

by
Vanessa Landry

Xulon PRESS

Dedications

This book was inspired by God's Holy Spirit!

My Heavenly Father, I dedicate this book to You for You were my inspiration in pulling this all together. Without You, none of this would or could have been possible. I am nothing without You, but I am everything with You by my side. For this, I honor and love You. Thank You for guiding me to this point and time in my life.

All praise, honor, and glory belong to You! I love You!

Secondly, I would like to dedicate this book to my mom, the late Rosa B. Robinson, who departed this life on November 29, 2005 and who is the love of my life and will always be in my heart, now and forevermore. Where would I have been without your guidance and love? You introduced and taught me to walk in the path of righteousness and to lean on God for all things. You were my best friend and I'll never forget you. Bone of my bones; flesh of my flesh. May you rest in peace in eternity where I will meet you again one day. When my purpose is complete, I'll be home.

Lastly, I'd like to also dedicate this book in memory of the late Bishop Stella "Victory" Mack who was Overseer of Holy Cross P.B.S Church, located in Capital Heights, Maryland. This woman was a great part of my life and influenced many changes in my life. She was a warm, loving, giving person; these qualities drew me to her side. She was truly a jewel to all of us who knew her. When I thought of Bishop's spiritual eyes of wisdom, I would not want to stray because I knew that God would somehow send her a fax! I remember the last words she sent to me, "Wait on the Lord." That is what I'm doing, Bishop! Still waiting!

Miss you!

CONTENTS

Poems

Words of Encouragement

The Man I Love

I think I cried when I wrote this one because of the love I felt for the Father. The greatest love you could ever know is the love of God. No human could ever love you the way God loves you. When I was in the world of sin, I searched and searched and could not find one as fine as God. It took me years to figure that out. When I did not know how to love myself, God took care of me. He kept me from all harm and danger when I had no idea of what might come my way. God scooped me up in His arms and taught me how to love myself. If I knew how to love Him first, I in turn could love myself and others with His unfailing love. Loving God is always the first step to loving yourself and others!

Matthew 22:37 *Jesus said unto him, Thou shalt* **love** *the Lord thy God with all thy heart, and with all thy soul, and with all thy mind.* **(KJV)**

The Man I Love

The Man I love is a great man. He sits high upon His throne
and looks low overseeing everything that I say and do.
The Man I love comforts me when I am down and there is no one else to talk to.
The Man I love protects me from evil and harm,
day and night as He surrounds me with His loving arms.
The Man I love shows up like a knight in shining armor and supplies all my need
through His riches in glory in Christ Jesus.
The Man I love would never hurt me
because He has a heart wider than the earth itself.
The Man I love loves me to worship and praise Him,
for this is what He deserves.
The Man I love?
You say, who is He?
He is the Most High God above!

Words of Encouragement

From Prison to Praise!

I was previously in an anointed choir at Holy Cross P.B.S. Church located in Capital Heights, Maryland. I wrote and recited this poem for our opening night release of the CD, *From Prison to Praise!*

This poem talks about how you should not always think of yourselves as the needy. We get so wrapped up in our problems and day-to-day situations, we forget about the lost sheep who need us to bring them home. If we are always complaining and whining to God, how can we be the strength that the weak man needs who does not know God as his Savior? We say we know Him, but do we really? Do we really trust Him for the things His Word promises, or are we prisoners trapped in our own way of thinking? If God said it, that settles it!

Come on! Get your minds out of prison and give God some praise!

Philippians 4:8 *Finally, brethren, whatsoever things are true, whatsoever things are honest, whatsoever things are just, whatsoever things are pure, whatsoever things are lovely, whatsoever things are of good report; if there be any virtue, and if there be any* **praise***, think on these things.* **(KJV)**

From Prison to Praise!

When I was in prison, I only thought of myself,
always complaining of having no money when GOD, was my wealth!
When I was in prison, I only thought of my sorrows;
I didn't stop to think about my brother who was unsaved,
nor the one that did not make it to see another tomorrow.
When I was in prison, it was hard for me to worship and pray,
but when I got into trouble, boy did I find a way.
When I was in prison, all those awful things in my life I went through,
I had no idea that those trials were tools used to strengthen me,
for God had greater works for me to do.
When I was in prison, I thought of the past and all I could have been.
I did not stop to think how God's only Son died,
to rescue me from death and sin.
When I was in prison, I sort of thought of things just like the world,
until God revealed to me that I was somewhat like that ole swine and the pearl.
You see, me being in prison, my spirit was locked in my flesh.
I couldn't get out. I had no idea I was so blessed.
I held all my hurt and my pain inside.
This only added to the torment and distress, I often tried to hide.
Tell me, what good was I to anyone being this way?
I was only deceiving myself and surely I was leading others astray.
But guess what? Now I can praise God and help tell others of His truth.
Before it is too late, I could help save some of the old and possibly some of the
youth.
So, people don't always be caught up in those things concerning you!
For God has others out there He wants us to spread His Word to.
Come on out of prison!! Come on out of yourself and give God the praise!!!!
Let everything that has breath, praise ye the Lord!

Words of Encouragement

No More Tears

This poem talks about how you should trust God for all things. He sent Christ to show you the way. Confess your sins to Him and ask Him to come into your heart and guide you with your life. He'll take over after that. He just wants your permission. Confide in Him when you have a burden and trust Him for your need. The wild animals even know to trust Him because they cry out to Him when they are hungry. What sense does that make? An animal knows what God can do for him when he is in need. No matter what the problem is, trust that He will make a way. The things of the world will get you down but wipe your eyes and know that God has it all under control. You'll see!

Revelation 21:4 *And God shall wipe away all* **tears** *from their eyes; and there shall be no more death, neither sorrow, nor crying, neither shall there be any more pain: for the former things are passed away.* **(KJV)**

No More Tears

Hey! I've got some great news to share with you all today!

It's about a man called Jesus who came to show you the way!

He died for the sins of the world so that you would be blessed. All He wants you to do is give your life to Him as you confess!

Tell Him all about those things that weigh you down. Trusting that He can and will turn those things around. Know that He has experienced all that you're going through. Yes, in spirit, He's walking and even talking with you.

No need to cry and worry about the things of today, for tomorrow He promises an even brighter day!

You probably say, *He can't help me; this situation I've got is one in few.* I guarantee He'll help, if you'd just stop listening to you.

Bind up that enemy and send him on his way. HE HAS NO POWER HERE! That's what you should say!

I can't begin to tell you all the things that God can do. It's no secret that He lives within and He also empowers you.

The lions roar for their prey and they seek their food from God. You can't even trust Him for the little things He's promised you. Don't you think that's odd?

He who looks at the earth and it trembles, who touches the mountains and they smoke! Boy, I can go on and on about this Man. He's no joke!

I would like you to wipe your eyes today and take God at His word. This man I tell you can do anything, anything; you doubting Him is absurd!

He's coming back for you one day, the church without spot or wrinkle. They say you will disappear from here with just one little eye twinkle.

No more tears,

No more tears,

Dry your eyes,

No more tears.

Words of Encouragement

The Mirror

This is a doozy! It's about how you can't see what you really are on the inside by looking in a glass mirror. That mirror can't show you your slimy, slick, arrogant, cruddy, lying, disgusting ways because the mirror only shows the outer appearance. We are like the "white-washed tomb," meaning we are pretty and clean on the outside, but full of iniquity and the smell of a dead man's bones on the inside. The Holy Bible is the real mirror. It will get down in those cracks and creases where you *stink*, and no one knows about the things hidden there but you. Sometimes, you don't even know the things hidden within. God has to create situations and circumstances or even put people in your life so that those ugly, disgusting ways will become apparent to you. God wants to clean you up on the inside, as well as on the outside, so that you can be what He created you to be for His glory which is all in your purpose!

James 1:23–25 *For if any one is a hearer of the word and not a doer, he is like a man who observes his natural face in a mirror; for he observes himself and goes away and at once forgets what he was like. But he who looks into the perfect law, the law of liberty, and perseveres, being no hearer that forgets but a doer that acts, he shall be blessed in his doing. (KJV)*

The Mirror

The mirror is a reflection of who we really are.
It will not change what we look like nor will it display that hidden scar.
The Mirror will show you the crumbs displayed on your face.
It will not go inside and reveal what is hidden or one's evil space.
The Mirror will show you your complexion, when it's dry and dead.
But it will not show you what's going on inside one's head.
The Mirror will show you what your clothes look like
all dressed up in your suit.
It will not display your attitude, which is causing all the hate and disputes.
I must tell you, the Mirror will not show you what is deep down inside.
Your actions will bring it out. Oh, you can't hide.
The Mirror can show you all of your tears.
It will not go inside your heart and reveal your sadness or your fears.
God's Word is the only thing that will reveal what lies still.
It will go deep down in your heart and soul, and show you where
you are ill.
The Mirror is not the one on the wall, or the one displayed on your table. It's the
Holy Bible which GOD has given if you're willing and you're able.

Words of Encouragement

I Got Away

This poem is talking about all the things that could have kept me dead in my sin and the things that could have happened to me that were observed watching others. Oh, but one day God spoke to me in a small, still voice and asked if He could come into my heart and be in control of my life, and I felt obligated to do so because of God's goodness and kindness towards me. When I sit back and remember all the car accidents that they said I should not have walked out of or the smothering incident that had me gasping for my last breath, I get teary eyed. When I think about how God kept me from situations that the devil had planned for me—situations I did not even know about—my soul cries out to the Lord. I truly have the victory because "I Got Away"! What about you? Do you feel the same?

2 Peter 1:3–4 *According as his divine power hath given unto us all things that pertain unto life and godliness, through the knowledge of him that hath called us to glory and virtue: Whereby are given unto us exceeding great and precious promises: that by these ye might be partakers of the divine nature, having escaped the corruption that is in the world through lust. (KJV)*

I Got Away

Not too long ago, I was dead in sin, not caring that God had made a way for me to be forgiven and live again.

I remember doing my own thing, not even considering the things of God. I was partying, smoking, drinking, and dating real hard.

I remember one day stepping over a puddle of blood from someone who had been killed. I saw so much of this go on, it didn't faze me; I didn't even get a chill.

I remember the day when my girlfriend who was terminally ill was pronounced dead.

I sat next to her crying and holding her on her hospital bed.

I remember the drug addict who shot dope in his arm right next to me on a bus. I didn't say a word to him as I watched because I was afraid. He appeared to be someone I could not trust.

I remember when a close friend of mine started giving me all kinds of slack. She never wanted me around any more, for fear that I would catch on to her smoking that awful crack.

I also remember being smothered almost to my death, then an angel walked into the room that day and allowed me to catch my last breath.

Whew, out of all these things that could have happened to me way back then, God the Father reached down and saved me from hell and sin. He came to me one day in a small, still voice. He asked me if I would live for Him or would death be my choice. I thank Him for this revelation and how it changed my life today.

He saved me....I Got Away!

Words of Encouragement

The Resurrection Power—He Got Up in Me

I'm talking about how Christ arose in me. The Christ that was dead in me because I was dead in my sin. I was living the life of the world's standards and not God's way. The Christ who died on the cross for my sins and yours, He got up in me one day. All those things that I thought meant something to me did not seem as important anymore when I got to know Christ as my Savior. He taught me to get to know Him, and He would teach me all those things concerning Him. He taught me that if I turned from my wicked ways, He would give me the strength and courage to continue in Him and that all other things were not as important as eternal life. I just knew I was living then, but I was really dead in my flesh! He turned on that light that was dim for so long and allowed me to see that I was nothing without Him! And going nowhere but to hell! Nothing, I tell you, nothing!

John 11: 25–26 *Jesus said unto her, I am the resurrection, and the life: he that believeth in me, though he were dead, yet shall he live: And whosoever liveth and believeth in me shall never die. Believest thou this?(KJV)*

The Resurrection Power—He Got Up in Me

I used to be a Sinner—dead in my flesh. My body was the coffin; it had my spirit in distress.

I liked hangin' out at the nightclubs looking my very best. Tryin' to find that special someone who would put my emotions through the test.

I can't forget the sex, drinking, and getting high for fun. What in the world could I have been thinking of? I was a simple one.

Worshipping and seeking God was not one of the things I chose to do. I could not find the time, nor did I want to.

I had all kind of problems, and I could not see my way, thinking I could handle them with the lies I told each day.

I even thought of murder once and as I look back today, Satan really had me going, for I was going astray.

Now I have no desire to live my old sinful way. You see, I found out about Jesus who came to set me free.

Jesus came and gave His life for the sins of the world. Yes, every man, woman, boy, and girl!

Jesus arose from the dead on the third day. His Spirit became life, so we could find our way.

Now, I walk right as far as I can see. Jesus broke the chains; they are no longer binding me.

I never knew how great life could truly be until I accepted Christ; He gave me Liberty!

The Resurrection Power—He Got Up in Me!

Words of Encouragement

Love God as Our Father

Worship Him in all that you do! Serve others as if you are serving Him. We should not always have our hands out for God to do for us. We should be asking Him what it is that He would have us to do for Him because we are really here to serve Him. If we spend time with Him, He will place His desires and thoughts in our hearts. God is a great God and should be honored as someone great!

John 8:42 *Jesus said unto them, If God were your Father, ye would love me: for I proceeded forth and came from God; neither came I of myself, but he sent me. (KJV)*

Love God as Our Father

When we love God as our Father, we won't treat Him as a servant. We will ask Him, "Father, what is it that I may do for You on this day that You have given me?"

When we love God as our Father, when we pray, we will tell Him how much we love and adore Him just because He is the Creator of All and the universe!

When we love God as our Father, our trials and tribulations will be taken gracefully. Knowing that He shall deliver us in due season or when He feels necessary because of what sin is in us that He is trying to get out of us.

When we love God as our Father, we should stroke Him with kind words such as, *I love You because You first loved me*, or just plain ole, *Hallelujah!*

When we love God as our Father, we try to handle situations and think as God would want us to think and do.

When we love God as our Father, we flee away from sinful acts knowing His eyes are upon us.

When we love God as our Father, we respect those in authority, knowing, whether they be good or bad, God is in control.

When we love God as our Father, paying our tithes will not be a struggle. You will be anxious to give back to God what He has loaned to you and then some.

When we love God as our Father, when we speak, sweet words of wisdom should flow from our lips as honey dripping from a honey comb.

Try some of these or better yet, try some of your own. You'll see; He will love you for the effort.

Love God as our Father.

Words of Encouragement

Hallelujah!

Hallelujah is the highest praise for all God has done for you and me! Well, just praise God because He owes us nothing else. He paid our debt with His life so that we would have eternal life. Is this not Good News?

Nothing else has to be said but *hallelujah.*

Revelation 19:1 *After this I heard what seemed to be the loud voice of a great multitude in heaven, crying, "Hallelujah! Salvation and glory and power belong to our God."(KJV)*

Hallelujah!

God, who formed the world by the power of His Word, uses His Word to teach us how to live in truth and by faith.

When I think of His goodness and all He's done for me, my soul cries out, "Hallelujah!"

God had His only begotten Son Jesus give His life to conquer all sin, sickness, and death for me.

When I think of His goodness and all He's done for me, my soul cries out, "Hallelujah!"

Jesus rose from the dead on the third day after His crucifixion so that I may have life everlasting if I choose Him.

When I think of His goodness and all He's done for me, my soul cries out, "Hallelujah!"

Jesus is my strength when I am weak, if only I submit to Him.

When I think of His goodness and all He's done for me, my soul cries out, "Hallelujah!"

Jesus promised to never leave me nor forsake me and that He would be with me until the end of time.

When I think of His goodness and all He's done for me, my soul cries out, "Hallelujah!"

Jesus sent a Comforter, the "Holy Ghost," to guide, teach, and mold me until His return.

When I think of His goodness and all He's done for me, my soul cries out, "Hallelujah!"

I sit in heavenly places with my Father when I give my life to Him and obey His will.

When I think of His goodness and all He's done for me, my soul cries out, "Hallelujah!"

Jesus went to prepare a place for me, and He promised to return.

When I think of His goodness and all He's done for me, my soul cries out, "Hallelujah!"

I love Him! I love Him! I love Him! HALLELUJAH!!!!

Words of Encouragement

Revolution

Set your mind on high! Turn from your wicked ways, which is what this poem, "Revolution," is saying. Make a change in your life today. A change that will be eternal and not temporary. A change that is internal and not just external. A change that entitles you to heavenly benefits and allows your soul to prosper! A change that allows you to be under God's protective covering against the evil one. A change that will allow God to use you for His glory and purpose. A change that allows you to be the head and not the tail. A change that allows you to choose not to be in bondage or sin knowingly again!

Revolution—make your change today!

Jeremiah 7:5–7 *"You must really change the way you live and act. Treat each other fairly. ⁶Do not treat outsiders or widows badly in this place. Do not take advantage of children whose fathers have died. Do not kill those who are not guilty of doing anything wrong. Do not worship other gods. That will only bring harm to you.*

⁷ "If you obey me, I will let you live in this place. It is the land I gave your people who lived long ago. It was promised to them for ever and ever. (NIRV)

Revolution

Renew your minds and put those old thoughts and deeds away!

Everything should be fresh and new starting today.

Vivacious should be your attitude with eagerness leading your path.

Only God can do this for you, if only you would ask.

Love must accompany this because this is the key to your new adventure too.

Undo all those things that are evil and unlike Him because God did not create you with that attitude.

Try to be quick about it because time is about to unfold;

It's time-out for all the foolishness, the things that hinder your soul.

Ostracize yourself from sin because to God, this is filthy and no good.

No one knows the time or day the Son of Man will appear. Oh yeah, He's coming back—just like He said He would.

Revolution—make your change today!

Words of Encouragement

You Are Never Alone

This poem says it all and was dedicated to one of my sisters in Christ who lost her husband. I wanted to let her know that she has a friend who is close to her at all times, in spite of the feelings she encounters from day to day. When the cards stop coming, the telephone stops ringing, and the visitors stop visiting after the death of a loved one, God is still there! No matter what hardships you may be going through, remember, "You are never alone."

John 16: 32 *"But a time is coming when you will be scattered and go to your own homes. In fact, that time is already here. You will leave me all alone. But I am not really alone. My Father is with me. (NIRV)*

You Are Never Alone

You may be feeling sadness every now and then, but child
let me tell you about someone who sticks closer than a friend.
He allows you to wake up to see another beautiful day.
Before I go on,
tell me if you know a man who will treat you this way?
He comforts you when you are sad and makes your heart oh so glad
He supplies all your need and keeps you from all danger and harm.
Girl, He's even got you wrapped in His loving arms.
When you call on Him, He is never too busy,
especially when this world puts you in an uproar and a tizzy.
Now, tell me if you know a man who will treat you this way?
I tell you, this man does all of this and you don't have to pay a dime.
You see, He paid the price for your sins and surely He paid for mine.
He died on that rugged cross a very long time ago.
Oh yes, he put His precious life on the line.
Our purpose is to worship and praise Him and He'll make the bad turn to good.
He will do everything that He promised, just like His Word said He would.
His blood is what saves us from being stained with sin.
Even though that is something we all do time and time again.
I tell you, I tell you, have you ever seen such a friend?
He will never leave you nor forsake you; all you do is believe in His Holy Word.
Don't you know who I'm talking about? Girl, haven't you heard?
He's the Alpha and the Omega, the Beginning and the End.
I ask you again, have you ever, ever, seen such a friend?

Words of Encouragement

God the Almighty

This poem, "God the Almighty," means just what it says. *God is greater* than anything you could ever imagine. He is the King of Kings and Lord of Lords! The Alpha and the Omega, the Beginning and the End! He created *all—everything*!

Genesis 17:1–2 *When Abram was ninety-nine years old the LORD appeared to Abram, and said to him, "I am God Almighty; walk before me, and be blameless. And I will make my covenant between me and you, and will multiply you exceedingly." (NIV)*

God the Almighty!

He who created the earth!

He who created all beings and things!

The clouds are the dust beneath His feet

He reigns from Heaven Above!

He has everything in His hands; what an awesome God!

If only you knew Him and could recognize His glory!

I heard a sermon once on how Jesus turned water into wine. Yes, God could do this to your life; it would be simply divine.

He'll give you hope day after day! Happiness and peace if only you would submit and pray.

When you cannot see your tomorrow, He will help you to forget all about your sorrows.

He's the God Almighty, who can do all things! Just put your hand in His, and He'll give you wings!

You'll be free as a bird and your burdens light as feathers! That's what God can do in any kind of weather.

No one has the power or knowledge to even comprehend Him. When you think of all His goodness, your mind will go into a spin!

I can't imagine where I would be, if it had not been for Him.

GOD THE ALMIGHTY! HE IS THE GREATEST, AND HE LIVES!

Words of Encouragement

Tricky Christians

"Tricky Christians" is a poem about how all who claim to be "saved, sanctified, and filled with the precious Holy Ghost" act when they feel that you are not on to them. We become carnally minded when we get complacent in our walk with Christ, and the devil steps in and tempts us to react to what is before us. We were purchased with a price by Christ on Calvary! We have all power if we would just seek God in our weaknesses! He gave us all that we need to defeat the devil, but do we always use what He has left as our inheritance? The other thing is, we have to realize when we are wrong. The Holy Ghost is our teacher, but do we always listen when He speaks to us?

Acts 13:10 *"You are a child of the devil and an enemy of everything that is right! You are full of all kinds of deceit and trickery. Will you never stop perverting the right ways of the Lord? (NIV)*

Tricky Christians

Tricky Christians go around tipping, trying to take a man, knowing that he has that wedding ring displayed on his hand.

Tricky Christians sleep around, all between the sheets; if they don't cut it out, they will surely feel the heat.

Tricky Christians can preach and tell the Word, and don't even practice it; it's absurd!

Tricky Christians go out all week and do the partying scene; they come to church on Sunday acting like saints as though they did nothing.

Tricky Christians know the Scriptures and will dot every "i," smoking, drinking their liquor, and still gettin' high.

Tricky Christians will laugh and smile in your face, while working with their voodoo, trying to take you from this place.

Tricky Christians shout up and down the floor and will almost knock you out in passing, without speaking, on their way out the church door.

Tricky Christians sing right in the choir, singing of God's precious glory and living a glorious lie.

Tricky Christians live with someone out of wedlock, acting like they're holy; that's a bunch of poppycock.

Tricky Christians wear their dresses long to the floor; while meeting that man at the motel, they say they went to the store.

Tricky Christians know just what to say; meanwhile God is getting tired of all this child's play.

Tricky Christians try not to be on display, but God will reveal them to you; He has His own special way.

Tricky Christians worship the devil—just look at how they live—while God is willing, able, and ready to eagerly forgive.

Tricky Christians, tricky Christians, those tricky Christians!

Words of Encouragement

Walking in a New Dimension

This poem is about trusting in God for this walk of faith. It's not about what you are going through or what you have been through. It's not about what is seen and unseen. It's always about putting your hand in His hand and taking one day at a time because you know that He has everything under control. Even when it gets rough, trust Him. As He once told me, "Stop looking at the wind." You can't see the wind can you? You can only feel it.

Ephesians 4:22–23 *You were taught not to live the way you used to. You must get rid of your old way of life. That's because it is polluted by longing for things that lead you down the wrong path.*
23You were taught to be made new in your thinking. (NIRV)

Walking in a New Dimension

It's not about where I come from, who or what I used to be; it's about living in the Spirit, in the Spirit where there is liberty!

It's not about the things I desire and still do not have; it's about the riches I have knowing God; He'll bring all those others to pass.

It's not about the problems I encounter that won't ever seem to go away; it's about how I handle those problems, confiding in God for the answers when I pray.

It's not about that brother or sister who surely did me wrong; oh no, it's about how I responded in love, to help us to get along.

It's not about how sick I've been and still I'm in pain; it's about the praise I give God while going through this temporary strain.

It's not about that big title which was given to elevate me on earth this day; it's about the little time that was given to the lost to keep them from going astray.

Certainly, it's not about the devil and how he's always on my trail…. It's about TRUSTING IN GOD. He must always prevail.

This is what happens when walking in a new dimension.

Words of Encouragement

A Mother

" A Mother" is a poem about being blessed to have known a mother who nurtured, loved, encouraged, and spanked you. Some did not get to experience that in a mother. Some lost their moms prematurely in life. Losing a mother could have been from death, drugs, life's tensions that caused them to stray away, or just plain ole abuse. It could have been so many things. If you are one of the lucky ones who have had the privilege of having your mother, praise God for her. This poem was created for a friend who lost her mother. When your mother is gone, God is that mother your heart longs for.

Isaiah 66:13 *As one whom his mother comforts, so I will comfort you; you shall be comforted in Jerusalem. (KJV)*

A Mother

A mother is someone who carries you in her womb for nine months. When you are born, she nurtures, comforts, protects, and also keeps you fed and warm.

A mother is someone you can go to when you have something special or personal to say; she will listen no matter what time it is, it can be night or day.

A mother, believe it or not, is your best friend; she'll teach you the lessons of life even if she has to do it over and over and over again.

A mother can make you smile when you are sad; she'll remind you of the good times and take your focus off the bad.

A mother grows proud of her children as they grow old; they become responsible adults with their own personalities and characters, all of which she helped to mold.

So you see, a mother, though she leaves you, is never really gone; the thoughts and memories of her love will always be in your heart.

She gave you life, love, laughter and reminded you that you were special. You can also do anything you put your mind to for God told us this from the start.

Oh yes, I tell you, she's the lady who holds the key, the key to your heart!

Words of Encouragement

Did You?

Is just a simple reminder of things that mean so little to one person but mean a lot to another. Did you ever stop to think about the need of someone else? God wants us to be thoughtful of one another as well as thinking on him for the things that he so desires of us.

Did You?

Did you forgive your brother who treated you mean? This is what you should do so that you may keep your heart clean.

Did you pray for the person who stole from you in a transaction? Give it to God; He will judge and give them what they deserve in due season that's for sure.

Did you apologize to the person who said or did awful things to you? It does not matter if they deserve the apology or not. God may be looking for your response before He elevates you to the next level in him.

Did you call your brother to encourage him today? I've found that a lot of times, people are hurting and just need to hear a kind word of encouragement to help make their day!

Did you present to a brother the gift of salvation through accepting Jesus Christ? That's your duty to bring others into the Kingdom so that they may inherit eternal life.

Did you give your loved one flowers today? It's what you do for them while they are living that produces flowers in their lives while still here. As my mom used to say, "when a person's nose and toes are sticking up, those natural flowers mean nothing to them. They are only for display." When they close their eyes, they can't see a thing.

Did you pray for someone who was lost today? We have so many in our lives who are lost and we ignore their cries.

Did you pray for the Shepherds over your soul? They also need your blessings to strengthen and give them insight on direction they seek from God to prosper the Kingdom with you in mind.

Did you tell someone that you loved them today? It does no good when they are gone away.

Lastly, did you seek God for direction in your life and also how to reach someone else in prayer? He would love for you to consult Him on any issue of your life and surely regarding someone else.

Ask yourself some questions. I'm sure you'll find some that need clarifying too.

Did you? Did you?

Words of Encouragement

Heart of Stone

This poem is about someone who was selfish, self-centered, and arrogant. He never cared about anyone but himself. We all have people who cross our paths in life, and we are placed in certain lives just for a season. It's not forever with everyone you meet. Some folk are just in your life for a period of time. When you plant the seeds of wisdom into their lives and no change takes place, you must leave that person so that their wicked ways will not transfer to your spirit. Someone else will come and water your seed. God does the increasing of the person's understanding and wisdom. If you are good, and you surround yourself with bad, eventually, you will become bad too. Your thoughts will become negative, your deeds dark, and your laughter will be full of greed. You must come from amongst those of this caliber.

Ephesians 4:17–19 *And so I insist--and God backs me up on this--that there be no going along with the crowd, the empty-headed, mindless crowd. 18They've refused for so long to deal with God that they've lost touch not only with God but with reality itself. 19They can't think straight anymore. Feeling no pain, they let themselves go in sexual obsession, addicted to every sort of perversion. (MSG)*

Heart of Stone

Joe was a man with a heart of stone. I figured he was hardened from his past, for he was always angry about something, never socializing with anyone. Yes, he was always alone.

Joe never had anything nice to say nor did his deeds not have a motive. You could bend over backwards to do nice things for Joe, but nothing would he return. If he did anything for you, it was for others to see. That's what I have learned.

Joe was the greatest liar, the best I've ever seen. You'd never guess by looking at him that he was this conniving and keen.

Joe didn't want to hear about God nor the things that God had done. He was so rude and uninviting, I felt as though he would shoot me if he had a gun!

I went to God in prayer and asked what could I do? God answered and said, "There is nothing, my dear; it's not up to Me or you. A person can only be helped when the person with the problem comes to the realization that he or she needs deliverance. I give everyone free will."

So, I guess until Joe realizes that he needs help, I'll go my way. Hanging around him could be detrimental to my spirit.

Words of Encouragement

Hell Is Real!

This is the place where the people who do not choose Christ over the devil, life over death, good over evil are going to end up. It does not matter if you have never done anything wrong in your sight in this life. It does not matter if you are loving and giving in your sight. It does not matter if you attend church and are active in church auxiliaries. What matters is if you have confessed your sins to Christ, asked Him to come into your life and become Lord over your life, and believe He died for your sins and rose again. He came so that we might have life and have it more abundantly. That is in eternity. We are to practice eternal living while here on earth. This place is just temporary. If you have not confessed to God, try it now. Read Romans 10:9–13.

Luke 12:5 *But I will warn you whom to fear: fear him who, after he has killed, has power to cast into* **hell***; (Gehenna); yes, I tell you, fear him! (AMP)*

2 Peter 2:4,9 *For if God spared not the angels that sinned, but cast them down to hell, and delivered them into chains of darkness, to be reserved unto judgment; 9 The Lord knoweth how to deliver the godly out of temptations, and reserve the unjust unto the day of judgment to be punished: (KJV)*

Hell Is Real!

Hell is real, I tell you; you don't want to go. You'd better get yourself together or that is all you will ever know.

Hell is real, I tell you; the fire and brimstones too. You think burning your finger is painful; wait until it's all of you.

Hell is real, I tell you; the devil and his crew, they sit around a big ole table and talk about how to destroy you!

Hell is real, I tell you; don't be no fool. Get right with Jesus now, honey, because hell has no swimming pool.

Hell is real, I tell you; people scream all night and day. Let me tell you, football won't even make you yell this way.

Hell is real, I tell you; it's dark, hot, and gray. Once you get there, it will do you no good to even set your mind to fast or pray.

Hell is real, I tell you; its channels expand day to day; there's not enough room to hold them for so many have gone astray!

Hell is real, I tell you; get right with Jesus today! Don't come calling Him later after He has warned you in this life to come walk His way!

HELL IS REAL, I TELL YOU! HELL IS REAL!

Words of Encouragement

He Will

Some of us read the Word and do not know what we should be getting from it. We read the Word and it is just that: "words." When you have established a personal relationship with God, when you read His words of wisdom, they speak to you. God's words of wisdom show you things unheard of. I've had many encounters with God this way. I might have spoken to Him about a problem I had and when done, I just opened the Bible. Not even searching for anything. As my eyes hit the middle of the page, there was the answer or a response to my situation. How can God do this at the right time so many times? How did my eyes know to go directly to that spot on the page where the answer was? It is His Holy Spirit which dwells, teaches, and instructs as we become humble with God in spirit.

Matthew 7:8 *For every one who asks receives, and he who seeks finds, and to him who knocks it* **will** *be opened.* **(NIV)**

He Will

When you open your Bible, ask the Author to open your heart and *He will.*

Ask the Author to reveal something new to you, that you may have overlooked before and *He will.*

Ask Him to answer a question for you that you may need advice on or guidance for and *He will.*

Ask Him to talk to you, oh so tenderly, and caress you with His words of wisdom and *He will.*

Ask Him anything, yes, anything and *He will.*

Just be still in His Word and *He will.*

Words of Encouragement

Still Standing

This poem was written for my twentieth class reunion. It basically talks about how God kept us through it all, even when we were being foolish in our sinful ways, and how He kept us safe, unlike others who did not make it to this point because of premature death. All the things that we have gone through up until now have molded us to be who we are today. God is still perfecting us all until His return.

Matthew 12:25 *And Knowing their thoughts, he said to them, "Every kingdom divided against itself is laid waste, and no city or house divided against itself will* **stand. (AMP)**

Matthew 16:28 *Truly, I say to you, there are some* **standing** *here who will not taste death before they see the Son of man coming in his kingdom.* **(AMP)**

Still Standing

I once attended a school called Chamberlain Vocational High. It was nothing like the larger schools in the area. It was small, warm, quaint, and loving. A place that you would always remember once you stopped by.

Chamberlain was a school where we all came together to learn a special trade. Some of us barely made it out, shucking and jiving in the halls and bathrooms, going to class faking it just to get a grade.

There were secretarial skills, barbering, and bakery to name a few. Oh, I can't forget cosmetology where the girls went to get their cute and inexpensive hairdos.

Our teachers were kinda special with the love and care they displayed. They were sort of like family expressing their concerns in voice and sometimes, their concerns were expressed to you in physical pain. Yes, we all knew that there were quite a few of them that would not put up with our mess and from some of them we had to refrain for fear of further distress.

The bruises we sustained from our teachers were nothing compared to life itself. They were trying to expose us to moral values, self-control, and respect. If we did not have our own agendas, some of us could have escaped that thing called "PREMATURE DEATH."

I know we all have endured some hardship throughout the years and, yes, a lot of unnecessary strain. I wouldn't take anything for those lessons learned and still I remain. Those lessons helped to shape and mold me and still I'm not done. The older folk tell me, "Child, you haven't seen nothing yet; you've only just begun."

God knows the beginning and middle as well as the end. He knew what it would take to make us responsible women and men. So, never worry about your tomorrow, nor sulk and complain about today. Just thank God for the trials and with you He will stay. It's all working out for your good; you'll look back one day and say, "I'm still standing."

Words of Encouragement

Home

It's a wonderful relief to know that you have an eternal home other than that doom called hell. Heaven is really your home which is prepared for those who love Christ. Those who sacrificed their lives to live and do things in God's will. Not those things pleasing to the flesh. Christ has prepared a place for us other than this place of residence. We think that the things we have possession of here are beautiful; wait until the eternal home is in view! Wow! We belong to the King of Kings and Lord of Lords! Our Father is *rich*!

> **John 14:2-3** *In my Father's house are many mansions: if it were not so, I would have told you. I go to prepare a place for you. 3)And if I go and prepare a place for you, I will come again, and receive you unto myself; that where I am, there ye may be also. (KJV)*

This Scripture is not talking about a visual mansion or dwelling as most think; it is referring to Christ Himself. Christ is bringing us to beautiful homes in heaven which means He is bringing us to rest in the Father. The terms in various versions of the Bible (mansions, rooms) all stem from the Greek word for *abode*. That is the Body of Christ (Romans 12:5) which is God's temple (1 Corinthians 3:16–17). "I go to prepare a place" means Jesus is building His church, the New Jerusalem (Revelation 21:2), opening up the way for man to be with God eternally. For Christ did not enter a man-made sanctuary but heaven itself (Hebrews 9:24, 1 Peter 3:22). These are not mansions as man visualizes mansions, but our bodies purified and prepared to live in God and He in us (1 John 4:15–16). "If I go" means death on the cross and resurrection; "I will come again" means the Holy Spirit lives in Christians (John 14:1–4) to prepare us for Jesus Himself coming in glory to bring us unto Himself (1 Thessalonians 4:16). Christ was leaving to prepare room for each of us that we may be with Him eternally (John 14:2–3). This place with Him is home; this world is not our home, just a temporary tent (2 Corinthians 5:1). Christians are members of God's household (Ephesians 2:19), and He makes "room" or a place for them.

> **2 Corinthians 5:8** *Yes, we are fully confident, and we would rather be away from these bodies, for then we will be at home with the Lord. (NLT)*

Home

Home is not the place where my address is displayed.
Heaven is my home and man it is laid!
Home is not the place where I go to the kitchen and cook my family their meals.
Heaven is my home where there is no need!
Home is not the place where I lie down to go to sleep at night.
Heaven is my home, where I won't need to sleep and there will always be light.
Home is not the place where I sit and relax to watch the big tube.
Heaven is my home where there will be no need to watch Jerry Springer, the soaps, and that awful news!
Home is not the place where I keep my jewels and worldly possessions.
Heaven is my home where those things are no longer needed or obsessions!
Home is not the place where pictures of family and friends are displayed.
Heaven is my home, where we will all be the same!
Home is not the place where my clothes and shoes are kept.
Heaven is my home; I'll be immortal in spirit; I won't need to get dressed!
Home is not the place where I share with my family and friends my nightmares and fears.
Heaven is my home, where there will be no more tears!
This place is just temporary for now here on earth. Have you been preparing for your new home? It's a place you prepare for where you won't even need a loan!
HEAVEN IS MY HOME!! I TELL YOU! HEAVEN IS MY HOME!

Let's Go to Church

Soul Food

Welcome! Welcome!

Welcome to our home. Holy Cross is the place where good food is served, food that is filling to the soul.

Bishop Mack is the chef here and serves all our meals with love. Her words are seasoned very carefully by the Father up above.

For an appetizer we've got singing and some praises too. Don't get full on that because the main dish is God's Word, which was prepared especially for you.

For dessert, we've got some pie. Now it's full of the Holy Ghost. You'd better get a piece of this before you leave. We serve this pie the most.

So, please don't leave here hungry! Come dine with us again. The food served here is so good; next time you come, please bring a friend.

Welcome!

What Is a Bishop?

A Bishop is someone God puts in control, to oversee the congregation and minister to their souls.

A Bishop is someone who holds God close to his or her heart; the relationship they share—as it gets closer—nothing or no one can tear apart.

A Bishop is like the shepherd watching over the herd of sheep, constantly guiding them out of trouble before they get in too deep.

A Bishop, I tell you, stays on the skyline with God both night and day, praying that He upholds us all until we learn to take heed and obey.

A Bishop is someone you can talk to when real trouble confronts you in this life; he or she holds you and comforts you and encourages you to put up a fight.

A Bishop is someone who will not put up with your foolish mess! You see he or she secretly consults God who instructs on what to do and what is best to say.

I tell you, a Bishop is like a large treasure chest washed up on the shore, full of rubies, pearls, diamonds, and much, much more!

Words of Encouragement

The Thief

This one is deep to me. Someone vandalized our church and stole a few items. As I kneeled at the altar, I asked God about how someone could break into His temple and take what does not belong to them? When He responded the way that He did, it made me think. Truly, the thief does walk through the door and rob God in view. Truly, the thief has no regard for what God has planned for His Kingdom. The thief is the one who does not help to keep God's temple up to par. Especially when things run down within the church and some of us are blessed with certain talents to improve those areas that need attention. "Offerings" does not necessarily mean "money" all the time. It means what God has blessed you with as far as talents, services and time. Give some back to Him. We should come together as in *Nehemiah 4:6, So built we the wall; and all the wall was joined together unto the half thereof: for the people had a mind to work.(KJV)* When you are in a position to help and you do not, you are also "the thief."

Malachi 3:8 *Will a man rob God? Yet ye have robbed me. But ye say, Wherein have we robbed thee? In* **tithes and offerings. (KJV)**

The Thief

I came to church early one Thursday night. It was dark when I entered, so I turned on the light. I noticed a lot of plaster scattered around on the floor in the hall. It was the pay phone; it had been ripped from the wall. I walked a little farther trying to discover more. I noticed the window had been bent in the sanctuary and the screen was lying on the floor. At that moment I had a funny feeling as I searched a few rooms more. I wondered who would do such a thing? Don't people respect church anymore? As I finished searching to see if all was okay, I kneeled at the altar, and I started to pray. I said, "Lord, who would do such a thing? Why would someone come into Your temple and steal from You knowing that You see all?" God then answered in a small, still voice, "The thief is not just the one who broke into the church tonight. The thief is the one who walks through the front door willingly and does not pay his or her tithes and offer services unto Me or my temple. The difference is, the thief that came in tonight forced his way in versus walking through the front door to steal." I thought, "Wow, that was deep." Ask yourself the question, *Are you "the thief"?*

Words of Encouragement

The Case of the Missing Angels

This short story is truly an absurd one! Yes, this is somewhat like "The Thief." How could someone steal from God and not feel shameful about it? Someone walked into His home and stole again! Well, all I can say is God made us all. We are to pray for those who mistreat us, use us, and abuse us. Even when they murder and steal, we are to love them and forgive because Christ shed His blood; we are forgiven when repenting. You see, a sin is a sin. There are no little sins or big sins. So murder versus theft….there is no comparison when measured by His blood and grace. The two sins are the same to God!

Ephesians 1:7 *In him we have redemption through his blood, the **forgiveness** of our trespasses, according to the riches of his grace.* (KJV)

The Case of the Missing Angels

As the church was being improved in certain areas, the ladies room had angels displayed on the walls as though they were flying. The angels matched the angel border that was also displayed in this room. As I entered the ladies room one day, I noticed that the angels were gone! All I thought about was someone bringing in a large purse to take those angels. It had to be planned and it was an inside job! Why would someone do something like this? Again, an act of theft in the house of God! I asked God to bless the person who took them if they displayed them on their walls at home. I asked that He would send a special anointing from those angels that would cause the person who took them to feel guilt and shame and to repent and give his or her life to Christ. The person who took them couldn't possibly know Christ to come and steal from His temple!

Besides, it's the principle of the thing!

Words of Encouragement

The Pulpit Isn't Sacred Anymore

This poem simply explains what it is saying..."The Pulpit Isn't Sacred Anymore!" Preachers, teachers, and those of authority within the church feel that because they are God's servants, they can do and say anything.

Warning: God has not forgotten because nothing has happened!

Ezekiel 44:13 *They shall not come near to me, to serve me as priest, nor come near any of my sacred things and the things that are most sacred; but they shall bear their shame, because of the abominations which they have committed. (AMP)*

Matthew 23:27-28 *"How terrible for you, teachers of the law and Pharisees! You pretenders! You are like tombs that are painted white. They look beautiful on the outside. But on the inside they are full of the bones of the dead. They are also full of other things that are not pure and clean. 28 It is the same with you. On the outside you seem to be doing what is right. But on the inside you are full of what is wrong. You pretend to be what you are not. (NIRV)*

Jude 1:4 *What has happened is that some people have infiltrated our ranks (our Scriptures warned us this would happen), who beneath their pious skin are shameless scoundrels. Their design is to replace the sheer grace of our God with sheer license--which means doing away with Jesus Christ, our one and only Master. (MSG)*

Jeremiah 10:21 *The shepherds of my people have lost their senses. They no longer follow the LORD or ask what he wants of them. Therefore, they fail completely, and their flocks are scattered. (NLT)*

The Pulpit Isn't Sacred Anymore

What about the message that came on Sunday from a pastor who sleeps with other men? He attracts members which all have the same gay spirit. Isn't this awful? Isn't this a sin? **The pulpit isn't sacred anymore!**

What about the article I read about the gay bishop that the congregation knowingly elected? Supposedly, others that approve of this behavior are planning to align themselves with like-minded bishops who tolerate homosexuality! What is going on? They worship what God? Leading people astray! Boy, do they have a lot of blood on their hands. This is what the Bible means about the "false prophets" who will fool the very elect. The God I know does not approve of this!

The pulpit isn't sacred anymore!

Someone told me a story once regarding a church they were attending where the pastor was having an affair with one of his members. They supposedly fell in love; I say lust! Well, the pastor divorced his wife to marry the mistress and the church gave them an engagement celebration! What is wrong with this picture? This is absurd!

The pulpit isn't sacred anymore!

What about the lesbian pastor who was chosen by several votes? The congregation did not know about her lifestyle but when they later learned, they had her status revoked! If they had not looked at credentials but sought God for the choice, they would have known that this was not the one. They heard another voice!

The pulpit isn't sacred anymore!

What about the pastor who makes one believe that he must pay for a prophecy? Don't people know that God's Word is free? You don't pay for a prophecy!

The pulpit isn't sacred anymore!

What about the pastor who steals members from other churches for his own personal gain? Looking out for his money and not caring who is in need and in pain.

The pulpit isn't sacred anymore!

What about the pastor who is single and/or married; he fornicates and/or commits adultery and has his women all sitting in his congregation? He only uses them for his own selfish gain.

59

They don't know each other as they sit amongst each other in the congregation, but he can tell them apart.

The pulpit isn't sacred anymore!

What about the priest who fondles little boys and girls? Promising them money and maybe little toys as he warps their world.

The pulpit isn't sacred anymore!

What about the pastor who pimps the congregation and makes them feel obligated to give him or her all their hard-earned money? If there is any giving, it should be for the Kingdom of God! That is surely where the money should go. The pastor wants a nice car, a home, a few exotic trips, and of course some clothes. Don't they know that God will supply all those things if they seek Him first and His righteousness?

The pulpit isn't sacred anymore!

What about the pastor who paid Caucasians to come to his church? He claimed he wanted a mixture of races. This walk is by faith! God does the increase if he would just wait!

The pulpit isn't sacred anymore!

It looks as though God's house has been turned into a den of thieves!

The pulpit isn't sacred anymore! I tell you, the pulpit isn't sacred anymore!

The Sucker

One day I was feeling down and blue. I consulted God about my problem for this was the only thing to do! As I started to cry and tell Him all about the problem that made me blue, He gave me flashbacks of my life and all He had brought me through. As I cried out to Him, I told Him how I needed to be encouraged sometimes because I was always the one encouraging others. I specifically told Him that "I couldn't even get a sucker when I was down." I was really crying hard. I got myself together and went to church. After the service was over, I proceeded to leave the sanctuary. Someone approached me and handed me a sucker! Can you imagine that? I laughed so hard, I don't even remember who handed me the sucker. All I know is that the last thing I said to God before I left my house was regarding a sucker. I laughed all the way home. I thanked God for making me laugh and showing me He cared in a little way. Boy, did He make me happy that day! He is an awesome God!

God does have a sense of humor!

1 Peter 5:7 *Casting the[a]whole of your care [all your anxieties, all your worries, all your concerns, [b]once and for all] on Him, for He cares for you affectionately and cares about you [c]watchfully. (AMP)*

Words of Encouragement

The Other God

This is an observation. I have noticed that a lot of people in the church—not knowing that they are doing it—create another god. They go to the pastor for prayer on things that they could pray for themselves. They worship the pastor and are at the pastor's beck and call. The people should be this way with God. I'm not saying that the pastor does not deserve honor, I'm just saying that it needs to be put in the right perspective. The church tends to put the pastor above God. They don't see it and neither did I until we lost our pastor and it was so obvious. The people scattered when trouble came to the church. God is not only available to the pastor but to you as well. That is why Jesus died, so that He might be an intercessor between us and the Father. We can go to the source ourselves in Jesus' name. The church looks up to the pastor because he or she helps make the Scriptures plain so that the listener may get revelation and one day use what is heard (become a doer) to walk that straight and narrow path instead of continuing that broad road. The church puts the pastor on this pedestal when God does not want anyone to be before Him because He is a jealous God. Do people not know that it is God using the pastor to give you such great revelation, and the Holy Spirit is who gives the revelation to the pastor because He is really the teacher in all things concerning God?

Well, just read the observation following this, you'll see what I mean.

Deuteronomy 6:14 *You shall not go after other* **gods,** *of the* **gods** *of the peoples who are round about you.* **(KJV)**

Galatians 4:8 *At one time you didn't know God. You were slaves to gods that are really not gods at all. (NIRV)*

The Other God

The pastor was out for two long years. It was against her will for God had to whisper in her ears. God knew He could get her attention this way. Things had to change for this was God's play.

God wanted to show her things deep that were right before her eyes. Of course Satan had people planted right there in the church. They were all in disguise.

As the months passed, the congregation started to fade away. There were all kinds of rumors of why they left or had to go another way. Some said their spirits were dying. Some said that the Holy Ghost told them to leave. Some said they would return once the pastor came back. Some said, "I'm gone only for a season." Some went to support other ministries, and some just went!

Why couldn't they just roll up their sleeves and get to work? For it was God we were serving anyway. To see all of this made me sorrowful and hurt!

As I consulted God on the matter, as I always do, He answered and said "The pastor was their God. This is what I wanted in view. If they were here for Me, they would have worked until the pastor's return. It was all for show. With their lips they said they loved Me, but their hearts and deeds were far from Me."

You say who was the other god? The pastor was the other god!

On-Time God

One Sunday morning after our service was over, I was asked to present the welcome address for the service to be held in the evening. I got nervous because normally I have ample time to consult with God for Him to give me what to say. But this time, I had nothing but three hours.

I went to my friend's house who lived close to the church and asked her to let me go into the room where the computer was kept so that I could have quiet time with God for Him to speak to my spirit on what to say. I sat and I sat. I typed and I typed. I did this for at least two hours. Time was running short. I had only one hour left to be at the evening service. Still, nothing came to mind. When it was time to wrap it up, I was frustrated because God had not spoken to me on what to say. Frustrated, I went downstairs and sat in the living room chair of my friend's house in the dark. I heard a soft, still voice say "From Prison to Praise!" Boy, did I get happy! That was a poem that I had written and memorized for our choir's CD release about two years ago. I began to smile at God and say, "All that time You allowed me to sit upstairs in that room, and You gave me nothing until now. You knew all along that it would be something that I had already memorized." I began to laugh. He was not late. He was right on time. All I had to do was trust Him and wait.

He's an on-time God!

Matthew 19:26 *But Jesus looked at them and said to them, "With men this is impossible, but with* **God** *all things are possible."* **(KJV)**

Gone But Not Forgotten

(In memory of the deceased E. L. Wyche Choir members)
We miss your lovely voices used in harmonizing with us unto the Most High.
We understand you had to go home to be with Him—way beyond the sky.
We are still down here singing and doing our part as thoughts of you continue in each of our hearts.
We cannot begin to tell you all the trials we've been going through. Life is not easy, but God the Father is still in charge, guiding us in what to say and do.
We often think of all the good qualities that each of you possessed. No time to think of negative things that can drain you and leave you depressed.
The E. L. Wyche Chorale would like those of you that passed to know how much we really cared for each of you and hated to see you go.
Hopefully, we'll join you soon when we are caught up in the air. It will be so good to see you all relaxing in your easy chairs.
Oh no! We're not anxious to see you; we'll be there in due time. Just hold some spaces for us in heaven, somewhere/anywhere in the line.
We're gonna stay right here and keep ministering in our singing and in our praise; yes, He'll come back to get us too, one of these ole days.
You are "Gone But Not Forgotten"!

What Kinda Ghost?

Some of the saints sure do a lot of shouting these days. They say they are saved, baptized, and filled with the precious Holy Ghost. The saints treat you worse than the people of the world. That can't be the Holy Ghost!

What kinda ghost would allow the saints to despise one another when one is doing great things for the Kingdom, not to mention great things for themselves? They talk about you behind your back and hug you and say, "I love you in Jesus' name."

What kinda ghost just wants to sit and feast? Not caring about the sinner that is possessed with the beast! No one wants to cast out the demons any more. They barely want to touch you to pray if you look like you have a demon in you! What happened to the old ways of the churches? Some things should not change!

What kinda ghost would have you shouting and peeping out of your closed eye at the same time? Not to mention the one that skips a beat while shouting trying to outdo the next guy.

What kinda ghost tells a Pastor to leave his wife for another man and then they move in together? That's surely not the Holy Ghost!

Do saints sue one another without coming to an agreement? What kinda ghost is that?

What kinda ghost would allow a saint to speak in tongues aloud without interpreting what has been said? God would not do that because He wants what He says to be edification, and He wants it to be heard. Sometime folk sit there that know what is being uttered and don't say a word!

What kinda ghost makes you a promise and does not keep his word? I've seen a lot of this in the church because some have promised me.

Church folk have the highest divorce rates these days. What kinda ghost would make a child of God divorce their spouse when they are supposed to be setting examples for the world to see? This just doesn't seem right to me!

Hmmmmm, but sometimes I wonder what they are filled with. Is it self, envy, strife, or something else? What kinda ghost?

Isaiah 63:18–19 *Your holy people kept Your holy house for a little while. But those who hate us have broken it under their feet. 19 We have become like those over whom You have never ruled, like those who were not called by Your name. (NLV)*

The Appointed Leader

Who's the leader? That is what is being whispered amongst the saints. Who has the vision for the church to go on? Who? The leader is always the one next in line. Sometimes the position is not given to the person properly, as it should be, but God is really in control, and He will make sure who gets the spot. Trust me!

Some fuss over whether they should have the leadership spot. Who did all the hard work and laboring for the people when the original leader was out? I don't understand what all the fuss is about?

When someone is appointed as leader by the original leader, that settles it. The problem is that the people did not want to receive the decision made. I don't understand what all the fuss is about! That told me that the people did not respect the original leader's decision. God's Word says that we are to respect those who have rule over us. God is the one who gives one person authority over another. When we can't respect our earthly leader, how can we respect and obey God? How? God will assure the right one is appointed!

> **Luke 7:8** *For I also am a man set under* **authority**, *having under me soldiers, and I say unto one, Go, and he goeth; and to another, Come, and he cometh; and to my servant, Do this, and he doeth it. (KJV)*

> **Luke 22:25** *And he said unto them, The kings of the Gentiles exercise lordship over them; and they that exercise* **authority** *upon them are called benefactors. (KJV)*

> **Romans 13:1** *Everyone must submit himself to the governing authorities, for there is no* **authority** *except that which God has established. The authorities that exist have been established by God. (NIV)*

The Wedding Beatitudes

Blessed are the two (Man and Woman) that become one!
Blessed are those that cleave to God, their spouse, and release all others.
Blessed are they that are equally yoked in spirit and in truth.
Blessed are they that always put God before every decision they ever have to make.
Blessed are they that bring forth the gift of children that are rooted and grounded in Christ.
Blessed are they that saturate their lives with God's wisdom and love!
Blessed are they that have been married for many, many years!
Blessed are they that die in Christ, for they shall live again!!
Blessed, I say! Blessed!

Luke 1:45 *And* **blessed** *is she who believed that there would be a fulfillment of what was spoken to her from the Lord.* **(NASB)**

Church Folk

What is wrong with church folk? They say the Lord told them to do something and turn around and do the opposite. If God sends you somewhere to do a job, why would you leave because of opposition? That is what the devil does when God gives you a certain position.

What is wrong with church folk? They just can't get along! They smile in your face as though they love you and stand before the congregation or behind your back and say things awfully wrong.

What is wrong with church folk? You miss a couple of Sundays from church and no one from church even calls?

What is wrong with church folk? They start more confusion within the church then the folk outside of the church!

What is wrong with church folk? The ones who pray long, lengthy prayers and lie with the same tongue.

What is wrong with church folk? They never open their Bibles until Sunday morning while in church nor do they attend Bible studies. Don't they know that these are daily regimens that work?

What is wrong with church folk? They even sue one another! Are we not supposed to settle things amongst ourselves because one day, the saints will rule the land?

What is wrong with church folk? The ones that just want to hold that church title. When you really need them, they are nowhere to be found.

What is wrong with church folk? They always want financial help from the church and never pay their tithes?

What is wrong with church folk? Walking away from their church home to join another without being dismissed!

What is wrong with church folk? Are we not supposed to be in the same body as in the Trinity?

Enough! Enough! I can't take no more! When are we going to get right before the King of Glory comes? What is wrong with church folk? What is wrong?

Isaiah 64:6 *We are all infected and impure with sin. When we proudly display our righteous deeds, we find they are but filthy rags. Like autumn leaves, we wither and fall. And our sins, like the wind, sweep us away. (NLT)*

Uncircumcised Tree

You, who sit in the congregation and practice voodoo! Putting hexes and curses on people because you have envy or strife! Why don't you ask God's forgiveness and get on with your life?

You, who are abusive mentally, physically, and verbally! Why do you pretend to be so subtle and sweet?

You, who practice homosexuality within the church! It's awful how people are deceived into thinking that they are something they surely are not.

You, who lie with the same tongue you bless God with. Get back on the altar and cleanse that tongue with praise and ask forgiveness!

You, who preach and teach and don't live a word of it yourself. You can't be representing God; the devil has you for hire.

You, who still fornicate and commit adultery in body and in mind! You wipe your mouth as though you've done nothing. God knows; you can't hide!

You, who think that you are greater than the next man! We are all created equal but just have different purposes here.

Why do you think and do these things? Why? You Uncircumcised Tree! You bear no fruit! You Uncircumcised Tree!

Titus 1:10 *For there are many unruly and vain talkers and deceivers, specially they of the* **circumcision.** *(KJV)*

Romans 2:25 *For* **circumcision** *verily profiteth, if thou keep the law: but if thou be a breaker of the law, thy* **circumcision** *is made* **uncircumcision.** *(KJV)*

That Thing

I was worried about a situation that I could not control. My thoughts wandered day and night trying to figure it out. Not knowing that whatever I thought would not make things right.

I rationalized the situation, every way I could. Why was I doubting God? I was making a hill into a mountain. It had me saddened and depressed. I had to figure out this thing that had me distressed.

I didn't want to think about tomorrow nor did I want to deal with today.

I never even told anyone because what could they do or say?

When I got my thoughts truly together, I went to God in prayer. He gave me this peace about the situation that I really needed to feel. He also helped me to realize that what I had to deal with was another step I had to take to reach another level in Him.

Yes, I had to trust Him totally for my growth to take place. I could not take the step alone, or I'd remain in my space. I had to let go and trust Him totally for my change to come.

God is truly faithful in His Word, but I had to be reassured in prayer.

Now, that thing is no longer an issue because I gave it to Him.

Mark 9:23 *And Jesus said to him, " 'If You can?' All* **things** *are possible to him who believes." (NASB)*

Godly Gossip

Godly Gossip

Did you know that when someone insults you, you are to pray for that person?

1 Peter 2:23 *When they hurled their insults at him, he did not retaliate; when he suffered, he made no threats. Instead, he entrusted himself to him who judges justly. (NIV)*

You are not to get upset with them because it is a spirit that makes them respond the way that they do.

2 Corinthians 12:10 *That is why, for Christ's sake, I delight in weaknesses, in insults, in hardships, in persecutions, in difficulties. For when I am weak, then I am strong. (NIV)*

You must not try to avoid the person for God gave us power to do all things through Him who strengthens us. There should be nothing that you run from. Running gives the devil authority over your life when you let him do what he wants to you and avoid the situation. Try loving that person and praying for him or for her. Why let the devil steal your joy? Fight back with love and prayer. Ask God to give you the strength to deal with the person who offends you, and ask Him to guide you in your thoughts and words when speaking to the person. No one should ever make you stay away from church or not come to feed your spiritual man. This is an act of the devil or the thief. The thief comes to "kill, steal, and destroy"! **John 10:10** If you know this, why let him do it?

Jesus came so that you might have life and have it more abundantly. The only way to have abundant life is to feed your spirit with God's Word. That is *life* to your *spirit*! When you hear the promises of God, you then gain confidence in who you are. You must know who you are in order to know what you can do. Who are you? Do you know?

Godly Gossip

Did you know that you were created for God's use and not your own pleasures?

Ecclesiastes 12:13 *Let us hear the conclusion of the whole matter: Fear God, and keep his commandments: for this is the whole duty of man. (KJV)*

When God blesses you with earthly things (i.e., house, car, money, talents), you are to use them for His glory. He does not bless you for selfish gain. Also, know that Satan can bless you too. He knows what it takes to destroy you, and sometimes he will give you your desires because he knows the outcome. Especially when you are not ready for them.

God is not that way. He will only bless you when you are spiritually mature to receive it and know that it is to be used to His glory and/or to bless others. Satan, on the other hand does not care. He is hoping when he allows you to have something that it eventually destroys you somehow, someway, somewhere, someday! If you are in tune with God, He will let you know the things that are good for you and bad. Sometimes God will allow the devil to have his way to test us or to see if we will do the right thing.

Psalm 139:23–24 *Search me, O God, and know my heart: try me, and know my thoughts: And see if there be any wicked way in me, and lead me in the way everlasting. (KJV)*

God also allows the devil to have his way to teach us things that He wants us to see that we can't with the bare life situations. God takes something bad and turns it into a good thing. Is He not awesome?

Godly Gossip

Fulfilling God's will is what He desires of you. He expects you to give up those things that hinder your blessings that He has in store for you. Did you know that when God speaks to you in your heart about anything that you have done wrong or are still doing and you do not obey, there is a consequence you must pay for disobedience? Most of the time He warns you before you even get involved with something out of his will.

Ezekiel 23:49 *You will suffer the penalty for your lewdness and bear the consequences of your sins of idolatry. Then you will know that I am the Sovereign LORD. (NIV)*

The consequence may not directly affect you, but perhaps indirectly. It could affect a loved one or close friend. In **2 Samuel 11**, remember when David committed adultery with Bathsheba? They conceived a child while Bathsheba's husband was out fighting a war. David conspired to have the husband killed and married Bathsheba so that he would not have to answer to the sin. He did not get away with what he did because the child when born became ill and died. Even though you commit a wrong and repent for it, God will forgive, but there is still a consequence to pay down the road for the choice you made. It is because you planted a seed. You must reap what you sow, whether it be good or bad. So, the next time you must make a choice about anything, please, please, think about it! And remember God loves you and honors His Word!

Godly Gossip

Did you know that the devil is a *liar*? Someone told me that when they sin, they repent and still feel convicted. You know who that is, don't you? Making believers feel guilty of something already taken to Jesus in prayer? Jesus does not make anyone feel convicted after repenting. You are forgiven of all your sins when your sins are acknowledged in prayer.

"*There is therefore now no condemnation to them which are in Christ Jesus, who walk not after the flesh, but after the Spirit.*" (KJV)

There will be times when you fall. Just get back up (repent) and get on the right track. So who does the devil think he is fooling? That is his job, to keep you down when you fall. Just let the Holy Spirit guide you in all your ways, and He will teach you all the things concerning you and God's will. The devil knows we serve a God full of mercy, love, and kindness. He is also a God of wrath and judgment when we are sinful, but that is another discussion. John 8:32 "*And ye shall know the truth and the truth shall make you free.*" (KJV)

Godly Gossip

Did you know that God wants families to stay families?

1 Chronicles 16:43 *Then all the people left, each for his own home, and David returned home to bless his family. (NIV)*

If you don't have a complete family in your eyes, ask God to fill that void. Ask Him to send someone in your path who will teach you to have family time. Better yet, ask the Holy Spirit to guide you himself; He is the teacher of all things when consulted. Some people don't like to admit that they hurt deep down inside from a broken home. Some are just hurt because both parents were there but not with them physically. They were always working, trying to make ends meet. Homes can become separated in that way too. Not being around. You can grow apart emotionally.

Here's a short story you will like. This guy and his family were having dinner, and he was always one of those people who had an appointment somewhere. He was a family counselor. He was always in a hurry. He noticed that he was late for an appointment in the middle of dinner; he got up abruptly from the table, and his daughter asked, "Daddy, where are you going?" He replied, "I'm late for an appointment I have with a family." His daughter then replied, "When can we make an appointment for you to be with us?" The man felt so bad, he dropped everything and stayed with his family. Sometime, we can be so busy that we hurt the ones who really need us right under our noses.

Take time for the family . . . God would want it that way!

Godly Gossip

Did you know that when God places someone in your spirit, you should pray for that person? God may be showing you things about them because you need to intercede for them. You don't always know why He shows you certain things in dreams or visions. When you don't understand and even when you do, just pray.

Job 32:8 *But it is the spirit in a man, the breath of the Almighty, that gives him understanding. (NIV)*

Daniel 7:15 *"I, Daniel, was troubled in spirit, and the visions that passed through my mind disturbed me."(NIV)*

God may be trying to get the person's attention Himself, and he or she is so preoccupied with the situation or problem that they do not hear Him. Most of all, they may not know the voice of God and may be confused about what to do. Sometimes it is a soft-spoken voice (the Holy Spirit) or it can be a voice of authority.

Did you know that when God speaks to you, it can be through someone or something else, a situation or circumstance? This is called confirmation. He will have someone speak of future events to you or He will have someone confirm something that you already know. Remember, if what is spoken never comes to past, then the person that spoke in your life was a false prophet. The bible speaks of those false teachers that lived as sinners and were known as opportunist. There was one incident in particular where the prophet was rebuked by a beast.

2 Peter 2:16 *But he was rebuked for his wrongdoing by a donkey—a beast without speech—who spoke with a man's voice and restrained the prophet's madness. (NIV)*

Let me tell you this; He knows where you are spiritually and will communicate with you where you are spiritually. He also speaks to you through reading His Word. You asks, how do you know when God is actually speaking? Always remember, when *God* speaks, it will always line up with His Word and His will.

Daniel 2:47 *The king said to Daniel, "Surely your God is the God of gods and the Lord of kings and a revealer of mysteries, for you were able to reveal this mystery." (NIV)*

Godly Gossip

Did you know that God wants you to set your mind on Him?

Romans 8:5 *Those who live according to the sinful nature have their minds set on what that nature desires; but those who live in accordance with the Spirit have their minds set on what the Spirit desires. (NIV)*

If you set your mind on Him, when the enemy comes, God's Word will rise up in you, and you will respond the way Christ would. That is what developing a kingdom mind is all about. In order for you to live the kingdom way, you must think in a kingdom-minded way. You must saturate your heart with God's Word so that it will spring up in you during your day-to-day routine, a confrontation, or difficult situation.

Hebrews 4:12 *For the word of God is quick, and powerful, and sharper than any two edged sword, piercing even to the dividing asunder of soul and spirit, and of the joints and marrow, and is a discerner of the thoughts and intents of the heart. (KJV)*

There is nothing new under the sun that God has not covered.

When you have the mind of Christ,

Isaiah 56:17 *says, No weapon that is formed against thee shall prosper; and every tongue that shall rise against thee in judgment thou shalt condemn. This is the heritage of the servants of the LORD, and their righteousness is of me, saith the LORD. (KJV)*

Think on those things lovely and pure! The one and only Jesus Christ.

Godly Gossip

God wants you to use the talents that He has given you to serve others, whatever the need may be.

Matthew 25:20 *The man who had received the five talents brought the other five. "Master," he said, "you entrusted me with five talents. See, I have gained five more." (NIV)*

This verse is talking about money. The servant used what was given to him wisely. God gives gifts and talents the same way. He does not want you to be selfish with them and not use them to bless others because you are afraid or because you don't know what to do.

Teaching by your lifestyle, worshiping God with your lifestyle, and witnessing to others about whom we serve and why is using your talents that He has given. Singing, exhortation, the gift of healing and interceding in prayer—to name a few—are all gifts.

Luke 12:48 *But the one who does not know and does things deserving punishment will be beaten with few blows. From everyone who has been given much, much will be demanded; and from the one who has been entrusted with much, much more will be asked (NIV)*

Well, if you are holding back on the things that you have learned of Christ, you will be held accountable. Are you using the talent(s) God has entrusted you with, or are you holding back because you don't know what to do? Well?

Godly Gossip

Did you know that God loves you to pray? This is how you communicate and establish a relationship with Him. He responds quickly, at times, and sometimes He doesn't respond right away. He may not answer you for years to come because

> **2 Peter 3:8 says,** *But, beloved, be not ignorant of this one thing, that one day is with the Lord as a thousand years, and a thousand years as one day. (KJV)*

It may seem like it's taking a long time but to Him, it is just a second.

Prayer strengthens your spiritual man. It also allows you to desire the things of God. You are applying a protective covering over your life filled with blessings when you pray.

> **Psalm 91:1** *He that dwelleth in the secret place of the most High shall abide under the shadow of the Almighty. (KJV)*

See, I told you. It says it in His Word.

Secondly, when you pray, don't always ask for worldly possessions. Try some spiritual requests. Let God know that you want to please Him and do His will, and you want Him to equip you for the job. Also, let Him know that you love and adore Him. These are things He loves to hear. While you are driving, or walking, sometime just say, "I love You, Lord." Hmmmmmmm, it's like music to His ears.

Lastly, remember when you make Him the Lord of your life and desire the things that He desires, He will give you the desires of your heart because the things that you will desire will be the things that He has placed in your heart from getting to know Him.

> **Matthew 6:33** *But seek ye first the kingdom of God, and his righteousness; and all these things shall be added unto you. (KJV)*

Godly Gossip

Did you know that you should honor God's house? It should be a beautiful, honorable place. Making it lovely and keeping it in good repair is what should be done with the money collected in tithes and offerings. I've seen people that invest in only their personal homes and let God's house get run down and neglected. If the church you attend is your place of worship, the upkeep is your responsibility too.

2 Kings 12:13 *Howbeit there were not made for the house of the Lord bowls of silver, snuffers, basins, trumpets, any vessels of gold, or vessels of silver, of the money that was brought into the house of the Lord. (KJV)*

God's house should be kept like a palace. You should never let anyone destroy God's property.

2 Kings 12:12 *And to masons, and hewers of stone, and to buy timber and hewed stone to repair the breaches of the house of the Lord, and for all that was laid out for the house to repair it. (KJV)*

When you see someone leaving trash, drinking, or eating, you need to confront that person in love about the value of the church and its appearance. When one person gets away with it, it's like a plague that spreads to others. When you see things untidy, and/or inoperable, you need to pitch in and do what is needed.

2 Kings 12:14 *But they gave that to the workmen, and repaired therewith the house of the Lord. (KJV)*

If the task is too big, you need to go to one of the church officers and inform them. God would be pleased to know that you cared for His home. Remember to help keep up God's home; it pleases Him.

Godly Gossip

You must forgive your brother for all things that he has committed against you. I know sometimes it can be hard to forgive someone for the wrongs he or she has committed, but God's Word states that you must forgive your brothers so that God can forgive you of your sins.

Mark 11:26 *But if ye do not forgive, neither will your Father which is in heaven forgive your trespasses. (KJV)*

Remember, in the Bible there was a man who wanted to be forgiven of his debt and was pardoned.

Matthew 18:27 *Then the lord of that servant was moved with compassion, and loosed him, and forgave him the debt. (KJV)*

But, when someone owed him, he did not want to pardon the man. He had no compassion and threw him into prison.

Matthew 18:29–30 *And his fellow servant fell down at his feet, and besought him, saying, Have patience with me, and I will pay thee all. And he would not: but went and cast him into prison, till he should pay the debt. (KJV)*

Was that fair? So when you don't forgive, how can you expect to be forgiven of your iniquities? Be merciful, as your Father is also merciful. Out of the ten commandments given, God's greatest desire is that you love Him with all your heart, soul, strength and mind. The greatest commandment is "to love thy brother as thyself" (**Luke 10:27**)

Everything you do in this life will come back to you whether it is good or bad. So, treat others the way you would like to be treated. When someone has done you wrong or hurts you, say to yourself, *"I'm going to respond to this person the way I would like them to respond to me"*. That's easy enough! It may not always turn out that way, but it will be like pouring hot coals on their head (**Proverbs 25:22**). Try God's formula, it works!

Godly Gossip

Did you know that God cares for you and that He has great plans for your life? That is why He wants you to obey His Word so that you may find out what your purpose in life is. Your destiny. That is the only way. You must be obedient or you will never fulfill God's plan for your life. His Word is the only map to successful living.

Proverbs 6:23 *For the commandment is a lamp; and the law is light; and reproofs of instruction are the way of life. (KJV)*

There is no other way. All other avenues lead to self-destruction. I'm not saying that all your troubles will vanish. I'm saying that when you are obedient, you will come out of anything *victoriously* because of the power from God's Word.

1 Corinthians 15:57 *But thanks be to God, which giveth us the victory through our Lord Jesus Christ. (KJV)*

His Word must be stored in your heart. So, if you want a good book to read, check out the Holy Bible. It's a book full of wisdom and power!

Godly Gossip

Jesus loves you more than you could ever know. He died on the cross while you were still in sin. Now, that is *love*!

> **John 3:16** *For God so loved the world, that he gave his only begotten Son, that whosoever believeth in him should not perish, but have everlasting life. (KJV)*

He wants you to die to your ugly sinful ways. Can you do that for Him?

> **Romans 6:19** *I speak after the manner of men because of the infirmity of your flesh: for as ye have yielded your members servants to uncleanness and to iniquity unto iniquity; even so now yield your members servants to righteousness unto holiness. (KJV)*

While trying to present the gift of salvation to someone, the person told me that they did not want to serve Christ because they wanted to live doing the things of the flesh. Huh! Truly they shall die and are dead while in their flesh.

> **Romans 6:21** *What fruit had ye then in those things whereof ye are now ashamed?*
> *For the end of those things is death. (KJV)*

Godly Gossip

Did you know that when Christ returns, those that are going back with Him will be caught up to meet Him?

1 Thessalonians 4:17 *Then we which are alive and remain shall be caught up together with them in the clouds, to meet the Lord in the air: and so shall we ever be with the Lord. (KJV)*

Did you know that He has not returned yet because He is giving those that are not ready time to get ready? He has also not returned because all the prophecies of the Bible must take place first. They will be the birthing pains of what is to come. Once Christ comes, it will be too late. Do you want to be left behind? This is the only time you have to get your house in order. Will you get it right before it's too late for you? Will you help the others that are lost?

Romans 15: 20-21 *My ambition has always been to preach the Good News where the name of Christ has never been heard, rather than where a church has already been started by someone else. 21) I have been following the plan spoken of in the Scriptures, where it says, "Those who have never been told about him will see, and those who have never heard of him will understand."(NLT)*

Godly Gossip

Did you know that you could tell God anything? He wants to be your friend.

Proverbs 18: 24 *A man that hath friends must shew himself friendly: and there is a friend that sticketh closer than a brother. (KJV)*

His name is "Jesus." When you repent of your sins and give your life to God, He listens to you because He does not want you to stay a sinner. He wants to be the person you confide in about everything. Why would you tell someone about your problems who cannot help you when all you have to do is come to God in prayer?

Isaiah 45:22 *Look unto me, and be ye saved, all the ends of the earth: for I am God, and there is none else. (KJV)*

You know, He's right because He also says that He's a God who cannot lie.

Numbers 23:19 *God is not a man, that he should lie; neither the son of man, that he should repent: hath he said, and shall he not do it? or hath he spoken, and shall he not make it good? (KJV)*

So this means that if He made a promise in His Word, then you are to believe it when you pray. Your *faith* will make it happen. There is nothing that He cannot do. Did you know that God could do all things except fail? It is not in Him to fail. He is the King of Kings and Lord of Lords, the Alpha and the Omega, the Beginning and the End! Tell a stranger. This is one thing He doesn't mind you gossiping about.

Godly Gossip

Can I tell you somethin'? I love the Lord so much that I can't think of hurting Him. That is why I repent daily so that I can stay under His protective covering.

Mark 1:15 *And saying, The time is fulfilled, and the kingdom of God is at hand: repent ye, and believe the gospel. (KJV)*

Mark 6:12 *And they went out, and preached that men should repent. (KJV)*

Yes, that's right. You sin unknowingly and should repent.

Acts 8:22 *Repent therefore of this thy wickedness, and pray God, if perhaps the thought of thine heart may be forgiven thee. (KJV)*

When I think about His goodness and all He has done for me, my soul cries out Hallelujah! Did you know that the devil does not care for you? All he wants to do is destroy you. He will use any tactic he can to trick you and try to make you fall. God is not that way.

God will take you in your sin and turn you around. He will make the old you a new you! He has the power to destroy us all when we are disobedient, but He doesn't. How can you not love someone as good as that? When you ignore God and harden your heart toward Him, He still loves you. The one you should not be afraid of is the devil. He roars like a lion, but has no sound if your mind is stayed on God.

1 Peter 5:8 *Be sober, be vigilant; because your adversary the devil, as a roaring lion, walketh about, seeking whom he may devour. (KJV)*

God said to fear the one who can destroy the body and soul.

Matthew 10:28 *And fear not them which kill the body, but are not able to kill the soul: but rather fear him which is able to destroy both soul and body in hell. (KJV)*

God has the power to destroy you and cast you into hell. The devil has no power like that. He doesn't even have the power to torment you if you stay close to God and use His Word as your sword. The devil is not omnipresent like God—everywhere at the same time. His demons do his dirty work. I love the Lord, don't you? He thought of it all. All we have to do is follow His instructions. That's all.

Godly Gossip

Did you know that when you are spiritually dead, God cannot reveal Himself to you? When you are a sinner, you are spiritually dead.

> **Proverbs 6:9** *How long wilt thou sleep, O sluggard? when wilt thou arise out of thy sleep?(KJV)*

That is why sometimes people cannot comprehend what God is saying in their situations. They are still carnal minded. They know not the things of the spirit.

> **1 Corinthians 2:14** *But the natural man receiveth not the things of the Spirit of God: for they are foolishness unto him: neither can he know them, because they are spiritually discerned. (KJV)*

When you were a sinner, God's words meant nothing to you until you accepted Christ as your personal Savior, and then the Holy Spirit started to reveal God to you as you read and studied His Word. Still, sometimes you cannot hear Him because you operate in the natural world. God wants you to renew your mind in the Spirit so that you can experience Him all around you in every aspect of your life. The Holy Spirit teaches you His ways and helps you to think and respond to things and situations as Christ would. That is why you must Study! Study! Study! *Awake! Awake!*

Godly Gossip

Did you know that God wants you to have powerful, meaningful relationships with others? Dominating someone is a form of witchcraft which produces bondage to the person being dominated. Christ came that you might have life and that more abundantly. (**John 10:10**) Christ does not dominate anyone. He always gives you the right to choose. So if someone wants to dominate your thoughts, actions, goals, and life, don't let it happen. When Christ set you free, you were freed!

John 8:36 *If the Son therefore shall make you free, ye shall be free indeed. (KJV)*

In **Ephesians 5:21**, the Word talks about submission. You are to submit to your fellow Christians out of reverence to Christ. When you show disrespect to one another, you are being disrespectful to Christ. God wants you to have nourishing relationships so that you may compliment one another and grow in different aspects of your lives. The three ingredients for a successful relationship are:

1. **Try not to possess self-centeredness.** Consider others and how the other person would feel or respond to a thing or situation.
2. **Exercise mutual submission.** Both parties should always submit to one another in conversation, deeds, etc.
3. **Love one another.** Please have love for one another. God says this is the greatest of all the commandments. Love your neighbor as yourself. Your neighbor is anyone you come in contact with during this walk of life.

Godly Gossip

Did you know that little is much when placed in the Master's hand? When you use the little you have to honor God, it will multiply. When you use the little talent you have, He will allow you to be creative with other things. When you share what you have, He will allow you never to want when you need. This pleases God to know that you trust Him with what is given to you. Yes, *trust*! Did you know that what you have is just loaned to you anyway? God loans your possessions to you because *all* belongs to Him. Nothing belongs to you. You are just a steward over the earth and your earthly possessions.

Psalm 24:1 *The earth is the Lord's, and the fullness thereof; the world, and they that dwell therein. (KJV)*

With His mercy and grace, He allows you to accrue the things needed to live and be comfortable. When you can't seem to see your way, know that He will guide you along. Even if you don't know, He will still be there for you. If you have faith the size of a mustard seed, God will be pleased. If you need Him, He will be there! Isn't that *great* news?

Godly Gossip

Did you know that God wants you to spend quality time with Him? At least some time every day. The time you spend with Him helps you to grow and become what He created you to be. It also allows you to hear what He wants you to know concerning your daily life situations or things forthcoming. When you spend time with Him, you are staying connected to the Vine.

> **John 15:5** *I am the vine, ye are the branches: He that abideth in me, and I in him, the same bringeth forth much fruit: for without me ye can do nothing. (KJV)*

You need to reverence Him and tell Him how much He is loved and appreciated and not always go to Him for your desires. What about His desires? What about what He expects of you? It is easy to give Him this long list of items to take care of for us. Try asking God, *What is it that I may do for You on this day?* If it is something that you feel uncomfortable about, ask Him for wisdom and/or courage.

> **James 1:5** *If any man lack wisdom, let him ask of God, that giveth to all men liberally, and upbraideth not; and it shall be given him. (KJV)*

Have you asked God that question today? *What is it that I might do for You on this day? Give me the desire and understanding so that I might know what You require of me.* Try it. He will be pleased for your efforts.

Godly Gossip

Did you know that God was concerned with every little aspect of your life? Right down to the clothes you wear? He cares for you more than you could ever know.

1 Peter 5:7 *Cast all your anxiety on him because he cares for you. (NIV)*

You can talk to God about anything. I go to God about *All* of my problems, especially when I lost my mom because it was too painful to bear. Today, it still is painful. No matter what the problem is or how I may feel, God always makes it feel alright. When you curl up to Him and saturate yourself with His word, you have no choice but to feel better if you plant His word on fertile soil. This means to accept what He has said in His words of wisdom. Not having a closed mind about the situation because God's word is true. This also is accompanied by faith. If you don't believe what He has said in His word, you won't feel good about your situation. So don't lose sleep over a problem or situation. Give it to God, and He will make your burdens light.

Matthew 11:30 *For my yoke is easy, and my burden is light. (KJV)*

Godly Gossip

I heard that Jesus will wash you white as snow. Can you believe that? He can take your filthy rags (sin), and they become clean. Better than that washing powder you use. No, He does not use Tide, Ivory Snow, Gain, or Wisk! He uses the Blood of Jesus and the Word of God to clean you up.

John 1:7 *But if we walk in the light, as he is in the light, we have fellowship with one another, and the blood of Jesus, his Son, purifies us from all sin. (NIV)*

Matthew 4:4 *Jesus answered, "It is written: 'Man does not live on bread alone, but on every word that comes from the mouth of God." (NIV)*

Yes, the Word of God. It will show you your dirty ways as you grow in the Spirit. Are you working on getting those dirty rags clean? God would like you to change your cleaning methods and try His. What will you get? Eternal life! It's guaranteed!

John 17:3 *And this is life eternal, that they might know thee the only true God, and Jesus Christ, whom thou hast sent. (KJV)*

Romans 6:23 *For the wages of sin is death; but the gift of God is eternal life through Jesus Christ our Lord. (KJV)*

Godly Gossip

Did you know that in the Body of Christ, we need each other? Yes, we do. You may be good at one thing and someone else good at another. We are to complement each other in our gifts as we work together in the Kingdom of God. We are not to be envious of anyone and his or her particular gift because God gave you what is best for you to bring Him glory. Just as our hands need the fingers, our feet need the toes. It goes on and on with the Body of Christ!

1 Corinthians 12:12 *For as the body is one, and hath many members, and all the members of that one body, being many, are one body: so also is Christ. (KJV)*

We are to help where the other lacks, if we have that talent or gift. God is pleased when we help in the Kingdom and teach others to be of service to the Kingdom too. We are actually working for God. It's not about serving the pastor. It's always about God and bringing Him glory and satisfaction in all that we do. Do all that you do unto God!

Godly Gossip

Did you know that children are gifts from God? Yes, they are truly precious. It is your job to grow in Christ's knowledge so that your children may be taught the things of God. Yes, as you teach them the truth, they will teach their children. The truth will become generational! Yes, that is what was intended in God's plan for all mankind in the beginning of creation, but Satan got angry when he discovered the blessings that you inherit when being obedient to God and His Word. Satan makes you think that you are "living" while in sin, but you are actually "dead and rotten" and on your way to hell. So, please, teach your children the things of God for the Word says in

Proverbs 22:6, *"Train up a child in the way he should go: and when he is old, he will not depart from it." The children will be blessed for generations to come. (KJV)*

Also, it's your responsibility and you are held accountable for them when they know not what they ought to do.

Godly Gossip

Did you know that when we disobey God, this saddens Him? I can't imagine making our Holy God sad. Well, if you don't know Him and His ways, how can you say that you don't disobey Him? You can't possibly know that. It's hard for those of us who know Christ not to disobey Him sometimes. You must spend time with someone to know what he or she likes and dislikes. Correct? You see, He wants you to obey Him so that He can get all the glory and the praise. After all, when you obey Him, the devil is defeated. Did you know that God gave you the power to conquer the devil? Well, He did, and He wants you to study and use His Word so that you can be aware of the tactics of the devil.

2 Timothy 2:15 *Study to shew thyself approved unto God, a workman that needeth not to be ashamed, rightly dividing the word of truth. (KJV)*

That is your power . . . knowing God and His Word! I found out that if you will just take the time, He will guide you through all truth.

Godly Gossip

Did you know that sometimes God has you in prison for His glory? Yes, being in prison is being somewhere or dealing with something you don't want to deal with. Have you ever been somewhere you didn't want to be, but God said you had to stay? Or, have you ever had to deal with a hardship because there was no other choice?

Acts 12:4 *And when he had apprehended him, he put him in prison, and delivered him to four quaternions of soldiers to keep him; intending after Easter to bring him forth to the people. (KJV)*

God allows these things to come into your life sometimes to teach you and show you your strength in Him. He uses those bad times to gird you and strengthen you for someone else who will have the same issues or problems one day. He also does it for you. Sometime he has to allow issues to come into your life to cleanse you of some filth. It is always God's hand that delivers you. We don't realize how powerful we are until we go through something, and we can truly see our capabilities through God's power.

Being in prison can also mean a lack of knowledge toward the things of God.

Psalm 142:7 *Set me free from my prison, that I may praise your name. Then the righteous will gather about me because of your goodness to me. (NIV)*

When you don't know God or His ways, you cannot see that He is doing something in your life. You also don't know how much power you have in Him. The devil can only do what God allows Him to do to you.

Revelation 2:10 *Fear none of those things which thou shalt suffer: behold, the devil shall cast some of you into prison, that ye may be tried; and ye shall have tribulation ten days: be thou faithful unto death, and I will give thee a crown of life. (KJV)*

You may take trials and tribulations as negative things in your life, but God's word says

Romans 8:28 *And we know that all things work together for good to them that love God, to them who are the called according to his purpose. (KJV)*

Godly Gossip

Did you know that when your loved one dies, the person who has accepted Christ as his or her personal Savior and believed that Christ died and rose again will rise too one day? Yes, it's true. Even though your loved one passes on, he or she will live again.

1 Thessalonians 4:13–14 *But I would not have you to be ignorant, brethren, concerning them which are asleep, that ye sorrow not, even as others which have no hope. For if we believe that Jesus died and rose again, even so them also which sleep in Jesus will God bring with him. (KJV)*

When Christ returns the dead in Christ will be the first to rise. The Bible tells us this in

1 Thessalonians 4:16, *"For the Lord himself shall descend from heaven with a shout, with the voice of the archangel, and with the trump of God: and the dead in Christ shall rise first."(KJV)*

Is that not great news? So don't fret over a loved one who went to be with the Lord! That's why we live and serve Christ, so that we may inherit the promise of eternal life! He's an awesome God; He thought of it all!

Godly Gossip

Did you know that God wants you to trust Him for all things? Don't trust in money, jobs, those worldly possessions, or people! Just trust in Him. He will be there when no one else is. When all the things in the land are gone, He will still be with you. He is with you always.

Psalm 139:7-8 *Where can I go from your Spirit? Where can I flee from your presence? If I go up to the heavens, you are there; if I make my bed in the depths, you are there. (NIV)*

If He takes care of the wild animals in the field, why would He not take care of you and your need? He knows what you need before you even know. HA! HA! Is that not funny? If you trust Him, you will obey and honor Him and His Word. If you have ever been on a roller coaster or in your car, you put that seat belt on, hoping that it will protect you because that is what man has said it will do. You buckle up, don't you? Well, in

2 Samuel 22:31, God's word says, *"As for God, his way is perfect; the word of the Lord is tried: he is a buckler to all them that trust in him." (KJV)*

Buckle up with Christ?

Godly Gossip

Hey! Jesus is the rock of your salvation. He is a strong tower in the time of trouble. You can hold on to Him and His promises no matter what.

Psalm 89:26 *He shall cry unto me, Thou art my father, my God, and the rock of my salvation. (KJV)*

His Word is firm and true. He is that solid foundation. The key to Jesus being your rock is giving it over to Him. "It" refers to whatever the problem in your life might be. Get out of the weary land and let God give you peace about it. You may be wondering, "How do I know that what God says is true and that if I give up all to Him, things will work out?" If you give it to Him, He has no choice but to take it and lighten your burdens.

Psalm 68:19 *Praise be to the Lord, to God our Savior, who daily bears our burdens. Selah (NASB)*

See I told you. He is sitting back on His mighty throne waiting for you to let go with His arms crossed. Can't you just see Him doing that?

Godly Gossip

In Job 38:28 God's Word states, *"Does the rain have a father? Who fathers the drops of dew?".(NIV)*

Well, the only one I know who could possibly father the rain and dew is God the Father of heaven and earth. Yes, He does this and bestows His mercy and grace on all mankind. That's how much He loves us and hopes that one day, those that are lost in sin will be found by receiving Christ before it's too late. He has no favorites so He wants us to be kind to those that are evil as well as the good. It's easy to be kind to someone because he or she is kind to you, but what about when that person is not kind?

Matthew 5:45 *That you may be sons of your Father in heaven. He causes his sun to rise on the evil and the good, and sends rain on the righteous and the unrighteous. (NIV)*

He awakens those daily who have found salvation and those who have not. He loves the evil as well as the good. He is so kind because of the hope we have in Him. So, what are you waiting for? He is waiting to become your Father.

Godly Gossip

When you do a good service unto God, please don't brag about what you have done. It does not please God when you do this. Sometimes people tell what they have done, hoping that they will get others to do what is good. There are other methods of sharing so that you can get others to reap benefits from doing good for the Kingdom. When you brag about giving a certain amount of money or rendering a service for someone, you have received your reward already. Wouldn't you like God to reward you instead of being publicly rewarded by men with their comments and praises?

Matthew 6:1 *Be careful not to do your acts of righteousness before men, to be seen by them. If you do, you will have no reward from your Father in heaven. (NIV)*

See, I told you; He will give you no reward because you've already rewarded yourself!

Godly Gossip

Have you ever heard people comment on why they don't pay their tithes and offerings? Most of the time, they are worried about what is being done with the money. Are the pastors buying houses, cars, boats, etc.? Sometimes, you will have hardships and can't pay, but you need to find a way; as long as you don't pay, you will never get out of your hardships because you are cursing yourself. That's right.

Malachi 3:8–10 *Will a man rob God? Yet you rob me. But you ask, "How do we rob you?" "In tithes and offerings. You are under a curse—the whole nation of you—because you are robbing me. Bring the whole tithe into the storehouse, that there may be food in my house. Test me in this," says the LORD Almighty, "and see if I will not throw open the floodgates of heaven and pour out so much blessing that you will not have room enough for it."(NIV)*

Don't worry about what is being done with the money because those that are in charge of the money, after they receive it, will be held accountable for what is done with it. No one will get away with anything because there is a righteous Judge who sees and knows all. So don't become a robber by not giving to God what He is due because someone else is not doing what they should do. Love God more and He will bless you for your efforts. Besides, you owe Him that.

Matthew 6:24 *No one can serve two masters. Either he will hate the one and love the other, or he will be devoted to the one and despise the other. You cannot serve both God and Money. (NIV)*

Godly Gossip

I hear people say that they are waiting on God to choose their mate. Let me tell you a secret. God will place many in your path for you to choose from, but He does not choose for you.

Proverbs 18:22 *Whoso findeth a wife findeth a good thing, and obtaineth favour of the LORD. (NIV)*

The key is lining that person up with God's Word. First, anyone you are thinking about marrying should have received Christ as his or her personal Savior. Secondly, he or she should have a love for God and have a personal relationship with Him. Some folk hook up before they know these things. Just because a person goes to church does not mean that he or she knows God. Knowing God is an intimacy you have with God in communicating in prayer and reading his word. Some folk have been in church for twenty-five to thirty years and still don't know who God is because they go to church out of religiousness and/or tradition. They go simply because that is what they were taught to do by their grandma, grandpa, mom, and pop. So what? You go to church on Sunday. Do you really know who God is and what He can do? What has He done in your life? How does He communicate with you? Some folk wouldn't know God if they saw Him coming down the street.

Your mate and you must be equally yoked spiritually. If you are not on the same level of understanding in the things of God, you will not agree on certain things and this can cause separation. You will experience separation in the relationship as well as with God.

2 Corinthians 6:14 *Be ye not unequally yoked together with unbelievers: for what fellowship hath righteousness with unrighteousness? and what communion hath light with darkness?(KJV)*

Amos 3:3 *Can two walk together, except they be agreed? (KJV)*

You and your mate should be one, not separate, in going to church and in decisions concerning God and His will.

Godly Gossip

Did you know that in every thing you are to give thanks to God? Yes, the good and the bad for He is in control of all. You see, He allows certain things to come into your path so that you may get closer to Him in prayer. Your trials and hardships are used as tools to help with things that you will encounter later on down the road. Your trial may be used to help another who does not know how to go through the same trial.

1 Thessalonians 5:18 *In every thing give thanks: for this is the will of God in Christ Jesus concerning you. (KJV)*

How can that be? Your trials make you stronger to endure more. They build you up where you are weak. You see, we are soldiers in the army of the Lord, and He has to mold and shape us to be what we were called to be. God knows just what it takes to build you up in Him. If you fail the test, you will have to go back to boot camp and be tested and tried all over again until you get it right. Yes. Trials and tribulations are tests authorized by God. A lot of times, we bring trials and tribulations on ourselves from being disobedient to the things of God. The devil goes to God and probably says, "Do I have permission to cause disturbance and trouble?"

Luke 22:31 *And the Lord said, Simon, Simon, behold, Satan hath desired to have you, that he may sift you as wheat. (KJV)*

Imagine God saying "yes" because He knows the outcome. See, it's all for your good.

Godly Gossip

Did you know that your body is not your own and that you were bought with a price? God wants you to save yourself for that mate that you marry. Your mate should have a love for God and a personal relationship with Him as well so that he or she will love you and not use and abuse you. If a person cannot love God first, he or she cannot possibly know how to love you because God is love!

Revelation 2:4 *Yet I hold this against you: You have forsaken your first love. (NIV)*

God has a reason for you to keep yourself pure for your mate. When you become intimate with someone, your spirit and the other spirits that you have united with become one with you in spirit.

1 Corinthians 6:16 *Do you not know that he who unites himself with a prostitute is one with her in body? For it is said, "The two will become one flesh." (NIV)*

That is why a lot of times we have certain desires in the flesh that we should not; the desires are there because of the uniting of other spirits. When you become husband and wife, you become one in spirit with each other as in Christ. You are no longer two because of the intimacy the two have and the binding of the commitment made in the sight of God. When you confess your sins to Christ and accept Him as your Lord and Savior, you then have a binding commitment and become one with Christ.

1 Corinthians 6:17 *But he who unites himself with the Lord is one with him in spirit. (NIV)*

So make God your first love and do away with sex before marriage. God would want it that way.

1 Thessalonians 4:3 *For this is the will of God, even your sanctification, that ye should abstain from fornication. (KJV)*

Godly Gossip

Have you ever been around people who have tried the "Get Rich Quick" schemes? I have. They do not know that the riches of this world do not matter because all of them will be gone one day. Only those things done for Christ will last and have any importance. People spend their whole lives trying to find happiness in riches. God is the only way to the happiness that is being sought by so many.

Luke 1:53 *He hath filled the hungry with good things; and the rich he hath sent empty away. (KJV)*

You see, this Scripture means that those who were hungry for the things of God were filled. The rich were not; they did not get filled with good things—the Word of God—his principles—and they left the same way that they came. Still wanting. Still not filled.

Luke 12:20-21 *"But God said to him, 'You foolish man! This very night I will take your life away from you. Then who will get what you have prepared for yourself?' 21 "That is how it will be for anyone who stores things away for himself but is not rich in God's eyes."(NIRV)*

Only what you do for Christ will last and fill you.

Godly Gossip

Have you ever had some real good soul food? Let me tell you, it is something good! I'm not talking about fried chicken or collard greens and corn bread. I'm talking about God's precious words of wisdom. His Word fills you up and makes you happy when you digest it well. You hunger and thirst for it when you are in a situation that you cannot control. A "weary land." That place that makes you sad and not focused on God and all your hope is gone.

Psalm 63:1 *O God, you are my God, earnestly I seek you; my soul thirsts for you, my body longs for you, in a dry and weary land where there is no water. (NIV)*

So you seek Him for guidance so that your hunger for Him may be filled. He gives you peace when you have been filled properly by accepting what has been said.

Psalm 63:5 *My soul will be satisfied as with the richest of foods; with singing lips my mouth will praise you. (NIV)*

Godly Gossip

Do you have a sweet tooth like I do? Well, I've got something that is so sweet that you just can't get enough of it. It takes the place of that chocolate, that strawberry, and that vanilla taste you have. It's soooooo good! It's God's Word again. Yes, It's Jesus and His Word that sweetens those things that taste like vinegar. It is an acquired taste!

Psalm 19:10 *God's Word is better than a diamond, better than a diamond set between emeralds. You'll like it better than strawberries in spring, better than red, ripe strawberries. (MSG)*

Godly Gossip

I heard that God hates certain things. These are the things that He hates and does not tolerate.

> **Proverbs 6:16–19** *These six things doth the LORD hate: yea, seven are an abomination unto him: A proud look, a lying tongue, and hands that shed innocent blood, An heart that deviseth wicked imaginations, feet that be swift in running to mischief, A false witness that speaketh lies, and he that soweth discord among brethren. (KJV)*

Remember, earlier I told you that there were consequences for the choice of sin? Well, when you perform one or more of these acts just mentioned, there is a consequence for doing so. God is a merciful and a loving God, but He is also a God of wrath.

> **Amos 2:4** *This is what the LORD says: "For three sins of Judah, even for four, I will not turn back {my wrath}. Because they have rejected the law of the LORD and have not kept His decrees, because they have been led astray by false gods, the gods their ancestors followed."(NIV)*

The other gods are those things that cause you to stay out of God's will. Yielding to your fleshly desires. So, don't have God angry with you about something. His Word is true.

Godly Gossip

Did you know that when you envy someone, envy eats away at you on the inside? The Word says it "rots the bones."

Proverbs 14:30 *A heart at peace gives life to the body, but envy rots the bones. (NIV)*

If our God blesses someone with possessions, a job, talents, we should be proud of him because he is our brother. What God does for one, He is able to do for another. All you have to do is ask Him for it.

Matthew 7:8 *For everyone who asks receives; he who seeks finds; and to him who knocks, the door will be opened. (NIV)*

See, God is faithful!

Godly Gossip

When you receive the gift of salvation, you are to tell others of the good news. When you don't tell others, it's like hoarding goods from those who need it. Yes, the Gift of Salvation is a great treasure for those who understand and receive it. Jesus traveled all the time to proclaim the good news as He taught His disciples who followed Him how to do as He did.

Luke 8:1 *After this, Jesus traveled about from one town and village to another, proclaiming the good news of the kingdom of God. The Twelve were with him. (NIV)*

Christ is also with us in spirit to help us proclaim the good news. Tell someone today who does not know about the Gift of Salvation. It's a great feeling!

Godly Gossip

Committing adultery is not just being unfaithful as with a spouse. It is also being unfaithful spiritually to the things of God. Yes, when you are disobedient to the things of God, you are committing adultery as well because of your unfaithfulness to Him.

Ezekiel 23:37 *For they have committed adultery and blood is on their hands. They committed adultery with their idols; they even sacrificed their children, whom they bore to me, as food for them. (NIV)*

When you trust in people, money, or jobs and not in God, this is idolatry because your trust is not in Him. Idolatry—trusting your things and other people—is insulting to God. He is a *great* God and wants to be acknowledged as same.

Conclusion of the Matter

Well, what's the end gonna be? Will you stay in bondage or will you be set free? Did any of the poems, short stories, or Godly Gossip sessions touch your heart, mind, and soul as they did mine as I prepared them for you? My heart is crying out for those of you who need deliverance in your life in some area. Maybe you don't trust God for what you have been hoping for. Maybe it's a healing. Maybe it's food, money, a new position at work. God can do ANYTHING but fail you! He is a God of "great promises," so don't insult Him with your little requests! Ask Him the IMPOSSIBLE and WAIT . . . He will answer.

Bondage is all the things that keep you from obeying the will of God and walking the narrow path of righteousness. When you are not obeying God, you are in *danger*!

> **Galatians 4:3, 9** *Even so we, when we were children, were in **bondage** under the elements of the world. . . . But now, after that ye have known God, or rather are known of God, how turn ye again to the weak and beggarly elements, whereunto ye desire again to be in **bondage**? (KJV)*

If you don't serve and obey God, you honor those things or beings that are not God. Those other things become your god! They are more important to you than the King of Kings, the Lord of Lords, the Alpha and the Omega, the Beginning and the End.

> **Mark 3:29** *But he that shall blaspheme against the Holy Ghost hath never forgiveness, but is in **danger** of eternal damnation. (KJV)*

Being set free encompasses all the blessings of God that give you liberty from obeying your earthly flesh and being obedient to God. For He is the one who created you for His purpose and His glory only! He does not force you to love, obey, and serve Him. He gives you free choice! He wants to see if you will be wise and choose life over death!

> **John 8:36** *If the Son therefore shall make you **free**, ye shall be **free** indeed. (KJV)*

Romans 6:18 *Being then made* **free** *from sin, ye became the servants of righteousness. (KJV)*

Romans 8:2 *For the law of the Spirit of life in Christ Jesus hath made me* **free** *from the law of sin and death. (KJV)*

Don't spend another night out with the frogs! In the Bible the frogs represented evil spirits, and they were used as a curse to plague the land when the people and their ways were not pleasing to God. In plain English, you are cursed when you refuse to accept Christ into your heart and change your life around.

Exodus 8:2, 7 *But if you refuse to let them go, behold, I will plague all your country with frogs. . . . 7) But the magicians did the same by their secret arts, and brought frogs upon the land of Egypt. (NIV)*

Revelation 16:13 *And I saw three evil spirits that looked like frogs leap from the mouth of the dragon, the beast, and the false prophet. (NLT)*

So, if you would like to be free today, please repeat Romans 10:9 aloud, "That if you confess with your mouth, 'Jesus is Lord,' and believe in your heart that God raised him from the dead, you will be saved." Be sincere when you do this for God is listening and knows all of your secrets. He just wants you to confess them to Him. Tell Him today! He is waiting for you with open arms. There is plenty of room to receive you! He does not care where you've been, what you've done, or who you are! He just wants to love you unconditionally! When you repent and ask God to forgive you of all your sins, then go find a church, if you don't already have one that you belong to. If you are in one, get grounded in His Word and learn of Christ and His ways so that you may stay on the path of righteousness. Say this short prayer and receive the gift of salvation:

Father God, I come to You as a sinner and repent of all my sins. I would like You to come into my heart, mind, and soul and cleanse me of all unrighteousness. I want You to fill me with Your joy, love, peace, and infinite wisdom so that I only learn of You and Your ways to fulfill my purpose which You have created me for. Forgive me, oh God, of all my unrighteous ways and lead me to the path of righteousness through Your love. I believe that Jesus Christ is Lord and that You raised Him from the dead so that I would have eternal life if I chose You. Today, I choose You as the Lord over my life. I thank You for Saving me in Jesus' name. Amen.

Repent and confess. . . .invite Christ into your heart and do it today! Tomorrow may be too late!

About the Author

Vanessa Landry formerly taught the Scriptures in Bible studies at Holy Cross P.B.S. Church, located in Capital Heights, Maryland, where the pastor was the late Bishop Stella V. Mack and presently officiating is Pastor Irving L. Rollins. Ms. Landry has been active in the church, ministering with her poems, encouraging cards, and gift baskets since 1996. Ms. Landry hopes this book of poems and short stories reaches a wider audience and also helps in encouraging and changing lives.

Printed in the United States
55060LVS00002B/361-588